When the Past Is Present

ALSO BY DAVID RICHO

Being True to Life: Poetic Paths to
Personal Growth (Shambhala, 2009)

Making Love Last: How to Sustain Intimacy and Nurture
Genuine Connection (Shambhala Audio, 2008)

Wisdom's Way: Quotations for Contemplation
(Human Development Books, 2008)

Everyday Commitments: Choosing a Life of Love, Realism,
and Acceptance (Shambhala, 2007)

The Power of Coincidence: How Life Shows Us What We
Need to Know (Shambhala, 2007)

The Sacred Heart of the World: Restoring Mystical Devotion to
Our Spiritual Life (Paulist Press, 2007)

Mary Within Us: A Jungian Contemplation of Her Titles
and Powers (Human Development Books, 2007)

The Five Things We Cannot Change: And the Happiness We
Find by Embracing Them (Shambhala, 2005)

How to Be an Adult in Relationships: The Five Keys to
Mindful Loving (Shambhala, 2002)

Shadow Dance: Liberating the Power and Creativity of Your
Dark Side (Shambhala, 1999)

When Love Meets Fear: How to Become Defense-less
and Resource-full (Paulist Press, 1997)

How to Be an Adult: A Handbook for Psychological and Spiritual
Integration (Paulist Press, 1991)

When the Past Is Present

*Healing the Emotional Wounds
That Sabotage Our Relationships*

David Richo, PhD

SHAMBHALA
Boston & London
2008

Shambhala Publications, Inc.
Horticultural Hall
300 Massachusetts Avenue
Boston, Massachusetts 02115
www.shambhala.com

12 11 10 9 8 7 6

Printed in the United States of America

♾ This edition is printed on acid-free paper that meets the
American National Standards Institute z39.48 Standard.

♻ This book was printed on 30% postconsumer recycled paper.
For more information please visit www.shambhala.com

Distributed in the United States by Random House, Inc.,
and in Canada by Random House of Canada Ltd

Design and interior composition: Greta D. Sibley & Associates

Library of Congress Cataloging-in-Publication Data
Richo, David, 1940–
When the past is present: healing the emotional wounds that
sabotage our relationships / David Richo.—1st ed.
p.   cm.
ISBN 978-1-59030-571-3 (pbk.: alk. paper)
1. Transference (Psychology) 2. Interpersonal relations—
Psychological aspects. 3. Psychoanalysis. I. Title.
RC489.T73R53 2008
616.89'17 DC22
2007048996

To all the Slubowski family
with gratitude and appreciation
for loving-kindness that began in 1942
and still cheers and comforts me now

CONTENTS

INTRODUCTION

The past is never ended; it isn't even past.
—William Faulkner

A poignant thing about us humans is that we seem hardwired to replay the past, especially when our past includes emotional pain or disappointment. As a psychotherapist, so much of my work involves joining people in noticing the ways in which the past is still very much alive in present-day relationships. Though most of us want to move on from the past, we tend to go through our lives simply casting new people in the roles of key people, such as our parents or any significant person with whom there is still unfinished business. Freud called this phenomenon "transference."

In transference, feelings and beliefs from the past reemerge in our present relationships. Transference is unconscious; we do not realize we are essentially involved in a case of mistaken identity, mistaking someone in the present for someone from the past. The term *transference* is usually used in the context of psychotherapy to refer to the client's tendency to see a parent, a sibling, or any significant person in the therapist and to feel and act in accord with that confusion. (There is also a phenomenon called "countertransference," which refers to the therapist's reactions to a client, especially when she appears to be a simulacrum of someone from his own past.)

Yet transference and countertransference are not restricted to therapy. Transferences from us and onto us happen in our lives every day. Unbeknownst to us, we are glimpsing important figures from our past in our partners, friends, associates, enemies, and even strangers. What we transfer are feelings, needs, expectations, biases, fantasies, beliefs, and attitudes. Transference is a crude way of seeing what is invisible, the untold drama inside us, or to use Ernst Becker's compelling phrase, "a miscarriage of clumsy lies about reality."

One example of transference is a patient falling in love with her physician. He is kind, understanding, reliable, and genuinely concerned about her. These are all the qualities she wished her father would have had. The patient might later marry this doctor and find out, as time goes by, that he is not what she imagined. Her conscious mind and heart believed she had found a replacement for her father. Her deep psyche, her unconscious, was quite adept at finding instead a substitute for her father. The doctor-husband turned out later in the relationship to be like dad after all, unavailable, unable to listen. The bond began with a transferred hope but became a transferred replay.

The enduring impression made upon us by significant relationships sets up a template that we apply to others throughout life. Our life is a theme and then variations that are never far off from the original tune. What chance do people have to be just who they are to us when we are comparing them to others while neither we nor they realize it is happening? What chance do we have to be seen as we are by others when they are transferring onto us?

Because of our natural tendency to twist our vision of others in accord with outmoded blueprints, it is only in rare moments that we see one another "as we in-ly are," as Emerson said. Most of the time, we are looking at one another through the lenses of our own history. There are two ways in which this can happen: (1) we might project onto each other our own beliefs, judgments, fears, desires, or expectations; (2) we might transfer onto each other the traits or expectations that actually belong to someone else.

This book is about our natural inclination, and at times our compulsion, to transfer and about how we can learn to see one another without obstructions or elaborations from our own story, even if only for a moment. Such clarity is a triumph of mindfulness, pure attention to the purely here. Unconscious transference gives power to then. Awareness of our transference gives the power to now.

Mindfulness is attention to the moment. Yet the moment is transitory by definition. So mindfulness is actually attentiveness to a flow. To live mindfully is not about a way of seeing reality as if it had stopped for us but flowing with reality that never ceases to shift and move. In transference we stop ourselves from flowing with present possibilities and instead stop to stare at a poster with a face from the past. We can catch ourselves in the act of placing our mother's face on a spouse or our former spouse's face on a new partner. We can also notice how others transfer onto us and we can find ways to handle their mistaking us for someone else.

When we engage in transference, we are attracted, repelled, excited, or upset by others. Our strong reactions of approach or avoidance may give us a clue to something still unsettled, still unfinished in us. Perhaps this person to whom we react so vehemently has reminded us of someone else, by physical resemblance or by personality. Perhaps he has released a feeling not fully expressed, a desire not yet satisfied, an expectation not yet met, a longing still shyly in hiding. It is called "transference" because we carry over onto someone now what belongs to the world back then. Indeed, as we look carefully into any present reactions, we inevitably notice a hookup to the past. "Introspection is always retrospection," wrote Jean-Paul Sartre. As we interpret our transferences in the light of our past, we understand our behavior in relationships.

Anyone who becomes deeply important to us is, by that very fact, replaying a crucial role from our own past. In fact, this is *how* people become important to us. They come from central casting and they pass the audition for us, their casting directors. We then make them the stars of our dramas. We don't call them "stars." We might instead call them "soul mates" or "archenemies." We are often sure "we were together in a former life." That is not so far off; we were together indeed, except it may not have been centuries ago, only decades or years ago. Synchronicity, meaningful coincidence, makes just the right actors come along for the audition. Our partners are then put under contract as performers, who gradually memorize the scripts of our lifelong needs or fears, and we may be busily doing the same for them. *Do I live in my own home or on a movie set?*

We might say, "We are working out our karma together." Yes, our bond in intimate relationships is often fashioned from the ancient and twisted consequences of our childhood or of former relationships. How ironic that those who matter to us have become stand-ins for those who, we might falsely believe, no longer matter to us. In reality, once someone is no longer important to us, his face becomes flatlined on our emotional screen and we no longer include him in our transferences.

Transference does not have to be seen as pathology but rather as our psyche's signal system, alerting us to what awaits an updating. Our work is to take notice of this and to face our tasks without the use of unwitting apprentices or surrogates. Unconscious transference is a hitching post to our past. As we make it conscious, it becomes a guidepost.

We engage in transference for some positive reasons. We are seeking healing for what is still an open wound. We are yearning for the sewing up of something that has long remained ripped and ragged. We try to complete our enigmatic history through our relationships with new partners, workmates, or colleagues. In this sense, transference can provide a useful shortcut to working on our past. This is healthy when transference is recognized, brought out of hiding, and used to identify what we then take responsibility to deal with. Finding out where our work is can be as important a purpose of relationship as personal happiness.

Transference is unhealthy for us when we remain unconscious of it and use others as fixit-persons for our troubled past relationships. We evolve when that past can find more direct and conscious ways to complete itself. Then others become prompters that help us move on in our story rather than actors who keep us caught in it.

Sometimes in our relationships we do step out of our old story with no need of a prompter. We approach someone not because she grants entry into our own unopened past or helps us forget it but because she is truly brand-new and only herself. This is the experience of an authentic you-and-I relationship. We approach a real person, not someone costumed in garments gathered from the trunks in our own attic. We then become more sincerely present with someone just as she is. This leads to the liberating possibility offered in authentic intimacy: mutual need-fulfillment and openness to each other's feelings. Our definition in healthy adulthood widens and deepens from the adolescent version: an attachment that feels good.

Transference issues can be baggage—the Latin word for which is *impedimenta*—or they can be fertile possibilities for growth. How sad it is that what shaped us became a burden and a secret too. Bringing consciousness to our transferences makes everything lighter to bear. There is no way around the past, but there are ways of working with it so that it does not impinge upon us or others quite so much. Our psyche's unrecognized operations can be exposed. The misreadings that are transference can become meaningful. Then the long longed-for restoration of our full selves can be consummated.

Transference is essentially a *compulsion* to return to our past in order to clear up emotionally backlogged business. We go back like restless ghosts to the house where the power-packed events occurred or, perhaps, did not fully occur as we wanted them to. The house we haunt is not our original address but the one we live at now. The people whom we haunt for fulfillment of our earliest needs are not our parents but partners, coworkers, friends, or strangers in our present life. Since all we have is the present, we use it to make up for the past. This is not wrong, only inaccurate. It is not a malady, only a misdirection.

We can expand our repertory for dealing with the past. It begins when we embark on a practice of *noticing transference mindfully*. We may then peer into the true nature of the unsatisfactory transactions of the past that yearn to fulfill themselves so desperately and futilely now. This form of mindfulness makes the unconscious conscious, the implicit explicit, just the technique that facilitates mental awareness, the psychological version of spiritual enlightenment.

Mindfulness is an unconditional awareness of the present without the clutter, conditioning, or contaminations of the past. We can deal with transference mindfully by bringing it into a present no longer conditioned by the past. In Buddhism, the here and now, when it is truly experienced, is ultimate reality. Our work on transference thus commandeers us to a high spiritual consciousness.

Transference smuggles the past onboard the present, and mindfulness escorts us safely to the port of the present, our illicit and burdensome cargo now cast overboard. Transference is an attachment to a fabrication, an illusion about others and ourselves. Mindfulness is its antidote because it is an accurate revision of others, of life events, and of ourselves as they are in this very moment.

Yet we have to concede that the present cannot help but hold some vestiges of the past. To be present mindfully does not mean living with no history—an impossible, useless, and dangerous task. We are mindful as we acknowledge our past as an inevitable and subtle stowaway in our lives. Then we are in the best position to update our ship's manifest. This takes the psychological work of addressing, processing, resolving, and integrating past events that still gnaw at us. It may mean grieving childhood relationships or finishing some emotionally unfinished business with a recent partner. It will certainly entail an attitude of enquiry into ourselves and our story. These tasks—all of which will appear as practices in this book—can be the psychological escorts into spiritual consciousness. Then we can sit mindfully in the present, finally free of ego and the stories that stop or drive us.

No one escapes transference. It is as much a part of a relationship as are apples to apple pie. In this book we find out how and why transference happens to all of us, what we can learn about ourselves because of it, and how we can come through it as awakened adults. We will keep an eye on the past, wink at our penchant for fantasy, and, hopefully, become loyal to the present. We sometimes take comfort in wishful thinking, a faux version of hope that does us no good. True hope is based on visible potential for change, a reality. Wishful thinking is based on projection, a concept.

Tattoos are carefully and consciously chosen and then needled onto the body. Our assumptions about, expectations of, and projections upon relationships, not consciously chosen, are tattooed into the cells of our bodies. The more a new situation resembles the past, the more bodily stress do we feel and the harder it is for us to release it. Yet, we can trust that our psychological work and our spiritual practice will yield physical results. We will feel our bodies relaxing, our breathing calming, and our tattoos fading. Transference, like all painful events, turns out to be an opportunity for healing after all.

In the chapters that follow, we will be surprising ourselves by finding out how many of our choices in life and relationship are tied to our own past—how much of what we call home is an archeological site. Our goal is to break the hold our ancient history has over us. Our challenge is to keep what is useful from it but to confront the ways it may be limiting our ability to reimagine ourselves and our relationships. Then we bravely join the poet Rilke in "the boundless resolve, no longer limitable in any direction, to achieve our purest inner possibility." What a thrilling prospect: to dare a bold escape from our karmic prison into the Eden of Only This, to dare a valiant leap over our past's detaining wall into the paradise of Only Now.

1

What Is Transference?

Learning to read, I stammered out, "See Dick! See Jane!" Did I ever imagine in first grade that it would take me another fifty years before I would be able to do just that? It has been hard work for me really to see the rosy faces of the Dicks and Janes I meet up with in life. It has required a steadfast allegiance to an unedited reality of who others are instead of falling into my habitual compulsion to project my own needs and beliefs onto them. It has taken conscious awareness of this person's presence here and now, free of my continual unconscious transferences from other persons, especially ones long since vanished into the past. I found help in the psychological work and spiritual practices I describe in this book. Now my vision of Dick and Jane has improved somewhat, or at least enough to notice when their faces are becoming blurred.

The word *transference* comes from two Latin words: *trans,* which means "across, over, or through," and *ferre,* which means "to carry." Psychologically, to "transfer" is to carry over the past into the present. We unconsciously place a parent's face or that of a former partner or any significant person onto someone else. We thereby re-create our childhood story or a chapter from a recent relationship. Transference is thus a perpetuation of old scenarios, an attempt at resurrecting the past.

The past tense of the verb *ferre* is *latus.* Thus the same Latin word is the root of both *transference* and *translation.* This seems appropriate since in transference we are continually translating the story lines of our own past into our present transactions. We are so often translating our childhood griefs or expectations, met or unmet, into newly arriving experiences with others. But it is ultimately the same book in another language. In any case, there are also those special moments with others in which transference is not at work, as we shall see.

The word *important* comes from the Latin *portare*, which is a synonym for *ferre*. Both words mean "carry." *Importance* is a metaphor for how we import or carry meaning into our experiences. Someone becomes "important" because he evokes a significance, makes an impression, has an impact on us. Originally, people became important to us because they had an influence on our development. For instance, our parents or brothers and sisters were important to our growth into adulthood. Our first spouse or partner was important to our growth in intimacy and adult love. In transference, new people become important because they mimic the originals.

Relatus, from which we have the word *relationship,* uses the word *latus* and extends the meaning to "carried back," a feature of transference. The word *intimacy* derives from the Latin *intimus,* or "innermost," the deep-within that we call the unconscious, another feature of transference. Thus, even linguistically, transference seems to be built into the concept of a relationship!

We can now attempt a definition. Transference is an unconscious displacement of feelings, attitudes, expectations, perceptions, reactions, beliefs, and judgments that were appropriate to former figures in our lives, mostly parents, onto people in the present.

Freud wrote, "Transference is a universal phenomenon of the human mind that dominates our relationship to our environment." He was echoing Shakespeare, who noticed that the world is a stage and all of us "merely players." People who become important to us play supporting roles in our daily drama. Perhaps their importance lies precisely in their ability to do that. How ironic that personal importance may not be tied to an authentic you-and-I experience but to a staged performance.

Freud further described transference experiences as "a special class of mental structures . . . new editions or facsimiles which . . . replace earlier persons." In transference we become caught in an anachronism, since we are replicating our emotional experience of childhood with someone to whom we are relating in the present. *Indeed, the word* present *becomes more symbolic than real once we realize that the past is so much a part of it.*

The frequency of transference makes us wonder if only the original characters in our life were truly significant and that others become significant later *because* they impersonate them. "You are special to me" may mean "You can play the part and if you cannot, I can train you for the role." The phrase "I married my mother" is the equivalent of "I found someone who fit my transference needs left over from life with mother."

The puzzle in therapy is not how did I get this way, but what does my angel want with me?
            —James Hillman

How We Defend

To understand our topic more clearly, it is useful to distinguish three terms in psychology: *transference, displacement,* and *projection.* They are unconscious mechanisms our ego uses to defend itself against stress. They can be healthy when they are used occasionally to help us over a fear or to stabilize and maintain ourselves. They become dysfunctional when we become possessed by them or when we use them to avoid looking at the truth about ourselves or reality. Here are the distinctions:

Carl Jung wrote, "Projection makes the whole world a replica of our own unknown face." I *project* onto another person characteristics, positive or negative, that I am unconscious of in myself; I shift onto others the traits, feelings, and motivations that belong to me. For example, I see you as controlling when all the while I don't notice how controlling I am. I may also project my beliefs about someone or about what someone feels. Projection mistakes an internal experience for an external one, a "you out there" for an "I in here." *In projection, I spend every day alone.*

I *displace* onto person B the feelings appropriate to person A. For example, I am angry at someone at work, but I take it out on my partner. Displacement mistakes one person for another, often an innocent bystander for a protagonist. *In displacement, I spend every day with the wrong person.*

In *transference* I displace onto others the feelings and expectations that rightly belong to my parents, family, former partners, or any significant others. Transference misplaces the past in the present. *In transference, every day is a family reunion.*

Transference is thus a type of displacement in which archaic family/parental transactions are reexperienced with other adults. Those others are usually confused by our behavior toward them because they do not see that we are inveigling them into a time warp. If they were to see our transference at work, they might pause, open themselves to compassion for us, and gently reassign our feelings back to us rather than letting them impinge upon them. Then our transference would become an assisting force in our personal growth, because we would notice from present reactions to us by others what is missing from our past.

In projection we believe that the other is thinking or feeling what we are thinking or feeling. The extreme form of projection is *identification*. For instance, you tell me you are lonely now that your relationship has ended. I understand how that feels both from my own past experience and from observing your pain. I imagine you feel/think just as I did when I was lonely. In that moment, I am feeling empathy, but I am also engaging in projection and identification, so I am not fully with you but rather with my own blend of you and me.

Perhaps empathy, and compassion as well, cannot fully happen without projection and identification? Freud referred to the use of defenses for achieving positive goals as a "regression in favor of the [healthy] ego." In this instance, we see mental constructs being used in ways that further the spiritual virtue of showing compassion.

Transference, projection, identification, and displacement keep interrupting the you-and-I moment, presenting their urgent bill from the backlogged accounts of our life story. Consciousness is the antidote to such a mistake, because it cuts through fantasies to arrive at the pure reality, no matter how disturbing or seductive. It takes courage and integrity to enter the unguarded present moment simply as a witness. One cannot be at the mercy of repulsiveness or attractiveness, of similarity or difference, of our story or of that of someone else.

How do we tell the difference between getting caught up in something or simply witnessing it? We sit on the beach as the clouds roll by. When we sit and simply notice them *without moving ourselves,* we are witnesses.

When we follow them with our eyes and crane our necks and perhaps see images in them, we are attaching to them, not simply witnessing them. A witness is one who sees without being influenced or determined by transference, projection, or displacement. He simply sees the bare fact with no editorial comment. His hands are in his lap, not stuck in the tar baby of ego or story. *To be stuck is to refuse to say yes to reality as it is and to move on from there.*

Getting You to Feel for Me

We can understand transference better if we look at one other unconscious defense mechanism, *projective identification.* A form of this happens when someone cannot stand certain of his own feelings because they seem too rude, too threatening, or too far out of character to know or show. So he does something that provokes his own unwanted or intolerable feeling in the other person, who in effect, feels it for him. We can see possible origins of empathy and intuition in this behavior.

Here is an example: I am angry at you but have always been afraid to show it, so I come late to meet you at the theater, arriving after the film has begun. You look and feel peeved and angry, so I get to see my anger but on your face! I am identifying my own feeling by having projected it through you. In doing this I may also be motivated by a transference need to re-create my parent's way of acting toward me. I may want you to act or feel toward me as my mother or father did. Maybe this time I can handle it. Maybe you will see what happened to me and ultimately feel compassion.

Inducing reactions in the other person that will feed a transference belief might also appear at work. I see you, my boss, as my critical father, and I do things at work that will lead you to criticize me. Now I revive my relationship with my critical dad or former spouse, of whom you remind me. I believe more firmly that I am an appropriate target of criticism, since you tell me so.

Projection and projective identification can be positive or negative. Sports fans imagine athletes to be living out their own ideals of competence and mastery. This is a positive projection. On the negative side, fans can rejoice and join by vicarious feelings in the violence they witness during an out-of-control soccer game. They are seeing the players express the rage they themselves feel. What a skewed and confounded search for mirroring. All this misdirected identification shows us that what we fail to integrate can become represented later by something else and we are then even more misled. This is exactly what transference is about.

We do not engage in projective identification because we are deceitful but because certain feelings are unbearable and we are seeking a safe way to diffuse them. We are not simply unloading our unacceptable or disavowed feelings. There is a positive—that is, developmental—reason. We are seeking a *model* for showing feelings. Then we can learn to practice feeling our own feelings safely. Thus, after seeing the scowl on your face at the movie theater—and noticing that you remain my friend nonetheless—I can learn how to show anger appropriately.

The person at the receiving end can practice *tonglen*. In this Buddhist practice, we take in the pain that the other finds intolerable, pass it through our heart-mind—serenely receptive and transformative because of our mindfulness and loving-kindness practices—and give it back in the form of healing compassion. This practice is alchemical in that it takes what is so unacceptable and turns it into something valuable.

In a sense, every time we listen to a friend tell us his troubles and respond with mindful presence and loving-kindness, we are practicing tonglen. We can say also that good therapy is tonglen, since the therapist takes in the pain and negative emotions of the client and gives back healing responses. Therapy thereby affirms how each of our feelings or attitudes, no matter how negative, can evoke compassion and lead to transformation. We then joyfully realize how every negative experience has positive, growth-fostering potential, how every liability is a resource, how every shadow trait has a kernel of value, how every disturbance or mistake can deepen our spiritual consciousness. The more we discover this truth, the less we need to project, displace, or transfer. There is an energy of light frozen in our confusion, a luminosity we can release, if only we do not give up our mining.

One of Our Habits

Our feelings about our current relationship may be conscious: "I know I am angry at my partner." But the origin and import of our feelings are often unconscious, as might be the attitudes and expectations beneath them: "I wanted him to speak up for me." Unconsciously, this may be "I expect him to be there for me just as dad was." Our fears or expectations usually grow from memories. Notice that transference can be based on positive memories, not only negative ones.

Transference is a habit in all people regardless of the quality of their parenting background. We will transfer whether our past was positive or negative in its impact on us. The fact that our psychic development is the result of a lifelong continuum of transference relationships may be a way of maintaining our own sense of personal continuity: "I am still with those I remember from my past, as long as I can transfer onto this new partner. He revives my story."

Transference is a homing instinct in the psyche. We all feel an urge to return to the past. Why would we want to do this? We are seeking a way to replicate and enact the unfinished business of our childhood or of our primary adult relationships. This inclination of ours can help us when it works to reconstitute the past so that we can explore what our hidden issues are and how they can be laid to rest. This happens in psychotherapy or in any moment in which we revisit our past and work out what is left of it in the present. It takes conscious noticing, catching ourselves in the act of transference, slipping out of the grip of the past, and what may be a fire walk into the real present. Psychological freedom happens when we find the courage to enter the here-and-now reality of ourselves and others, shorn of the decorations and detritus of our history.

Noticing our transferences may not be so difficult, since we choose people on whom to transfer that really do resemble our parents or other significant characters in our life story. We can gradually recognize—as will others regarding us—the similarities that made certain people such well-qualified candidates for transference.

Indeed, we can piece together our childhood history from the crypt of our unconscious. We do this by observing our needs and expectations in relationship and the partners we choose or keep choosing. We can also learn about our childhood from our patterns in relationships. For example, if our mother left us early in life, did we believe we made her leave, perhaps because we were not enough for her? Do we now make partners leave to repeat that scenario, mistakenly believing that repetition will be a completion? Do we hope they will come back as Mom did not? And if they do, will this mean that Mom's disappearance has finally been canceled?

Transference is a redirection of unresolved energy toward a safer object. We seek such a refuge since perhaps we may have felt the energy of the past to be too dangerous for us to confront directly. Thus transference, used to track our personal issues, can serve as a kindly scout that leads us gently into a territory that may be scary. This spouse can be more safely confronted than a devouring mother. Our anger, so terrifying to express in our childhood, can now be safely released in our committed marriage.

The safer object can be a stranger who annoys us, a colleague who snubs us, someone we are becoming interested in, an old flame returned, a family member or friend. All that is required for transference to kick in is some momentary gesture, word, deed, or manner that unconsciously recalls a person from our past with whom things are still unsettled. This may explain immediate attraction or repulsion. When we just don't like or definitely do like someone and we don't know why, transference may be at work.

Transference not only distorts who others are, it distorts who we think we are. Thus, the whole book of our life is mistranslated in transference. Consciousness is the new revised version that matches reality more accurately than the earlier texts. A fealty to what is real here and now radically opens us and widens our understanding of ourselves and others. We see the new newly and know others clearly, perhaps for the first time. It takes us such a long time to see. But that is nothing to be ashamed of. It is how the psyche works. All our ways of seeing the world are screened and stunted by our past until the rare moment of opening happens. Then a new inner landscape opens and we find our place in it.

At the same time, it is not simply a choice between authentic reality and a misrepresentative transference. We are usually engaged in both at once, since our past and present relationships are truly similar. A transference may thus not be totally a distortion, since there were indeed so many ambiguities in our relationships with the people in our past and now so many similarities to those in the present. It is well-nigh impossible to be clear about who is who. We find it hard to be precise about who people really are and what they mean to us in themselves. We therefore may refer to transference as a distortion only in the objective sense. Subjectively, it is not so much a distortion as a near miss, an approximation, a rough estimate, a ballpark figure—like so many of the beliefs and opinions we imagine to be gospel.

In the traditional view, distortion happens when a perception does not correspond to reality. With regard to others, we then fail to see a person, instead seeing only our subjective version of her. Our work then is to match our perception to her reality. But this may require an arduous climb rather than an immediate grasp. We can instead learn to know someone by engaging with her at gradually unfolding levels. We can keep finding out more about who she is while never quite knowing her fully. Then all it takes on our part is ever more generous receptiveness to who she is and ever more patience with a timing that eludes our jurisdiction.

Our story/transferences add weight to the impact of events. For instance, if someone does not make time for us, we might simply notice it and work around it, while there may also be some impact on our feelings. If, however, this is reminiscent of how unavailable our mother was in childhood, we might feel the blow more heavily. We then become more angry than fits the present circumstance. Some of that anger is part of the grief about what we missed out on long ago. As we notice a connection to our past, we see how the recent event helped us locate a long-unnoticed issue. We might eventually see that finding that piece of unfinished business is more valuable than being made time for!

Once we work out our issue, the world and others become just who they are. Then we can appreciate those who make time for us and, at the same time, say yes to the given of life that not everyone will do so. We might notice how we have been manipulating others over the years to make time for us. We give that up too. In any case, the fact that we were still looking for what we missed in childhood is a better position to be in than to have given up hope altogether. In fact, if the continuing search is what finally woke us up to transference, it has great value.

We do not eliminate transference; we decant it. We do not kill it as David killed Goliath. We wrestle with it respectfully as did Jacob with the angel, until it yields its blessing. The blessing is the revelation of what we missed or lost and the grace to grieve it rather than transfer it. We feel a momentum to mourn all those who did not make time for us, to let go of their importance to us, to go on with life no longer determined or unduly influenced by what others choose to do. We then find satisfying sources of need-fulfillment in ourselves and in other humans who can be there for us most of the time and not there sometimes. And in a yes to that, we have all we need.

In grief, there is an element of inconsolability. In our needs, there is an element of unsatisfiability. In the face of life's most profound questions, there is an unknowability. This fits with the work of Kurt Gödel, the Czech mathematician, who confirmed the "incompleteness theorem," which states that in any mathematical system there are indeed propositions that can neither be proved nor disproved. These natural incompletions reflect the first noble truth of Buddhism about the enduring and ineradicable unsatisfactoriness of all experience. This is not only Buddha's truth, it is the one that some of our children and punk rockers also proclaim.

Yet there is a positive side. Inconsolability means we cannot forget but always cherish those we loved. Unsatisfiability means we have a motivation to transcend our immediate desires. Unknowability means we grow in our sense of wonder and imagination. Indeed, answers close us, but questions open us. In accepting the given of the first noble truth without protest, blame, or recourse to an escape to which we can attach, we win all the way around.

Our realization about the ultimate inadequacy/unsatisfactoriness in life does not have to be a cause of suffering. We can relax into the transitory as natural. We can acknowledge that we are often easy to please but hard to satisfy. We can be content with *moments* of satisfaction, moments of fulfillment, moments of completion. We can notice that satisfaction with what is, in all its temporariness and unsatisfactoriness, grants us a liberating serenity.

The essence of ego-ignorance is its ongoing feud with the givens of life. Our unconditional yes to them lets moments be enough. We can then be like kaleidoscopes, joyous as stunning new designs appear and serene as they make way for other ones, even those not quite as stupendous. We recall the words of the ancient Greek poet Pindar: "Do not attempt to become Zeus; you have it all when just a *share* of beauty comes to you."

The Birth of Our Expectations

Transference happens when the past intrudes upon the present. One same way of relating is carried forward from decade to decade, from relationship to relationship. Our template from childhood can be so ingrained that we cannot see our present partner clearly. If mom was always loving, we might expect that same quality of love from a narcissistic partner who is unable to provide it. Our loyalty to the template may make us try to force-fit the glass slipper onto the wrong woman: "My experience with my controlling mother makes you seem more controlling than you are, and my wish for a kindly mother makes me hope you will be that way toward me."

A lack of love from a partner, resembling the lack of love from a parent, may lead us to despair that all we will ever be able to find in others is failed attunement to our needs. This is transferring our original despair onto the world. But, as we shall see, the failure of others may not be so bad. It may be just what we need to help us work on ourselves by dealing with our old hurts on our own.

A lack of love means not receiving the five A's of adult love: *attention, acceptance, appreciation, affection,* and *allowing* us to be ourselves. When we were not fulfilled in the past, we might seek those same five A's from others, a reasonable direction to take. But without working on ourselves first, for example, by grieving our past, we are likely to solicit need-fulfillment from others with restlessness and compulsion. That spells out as a must-have energy from us that may turn off prospective partners. Transference can then be an obstacle to relationship. The more we can become conscious of our transferences, the more apt we are to find out what we need to work on ourselves, to lay our ancient hungers to rest, to seek out those who can be more effective at loving us. Our whole style becomes less pressured and more relaxed.

Eventually we see that we can't be other than what we are and that means what we are must be just what we need to find fulfillment and just what the world needs as our contribution. Being ourselves is good news to the universe.

Wanting the five A's is not a sign of weakness nor a sign that a lot was missing in the past. It is always legitimate to want to be appreciated or prized, for instance. It is a sign of health when we acknowledge the legitimacy of our longings. That self-acceptance may settle into us as a *physical* sensation. It is akin to the special moment that occurs when learning to ride a bike. After falls and awkwardness we suddenly achieve a sense of balance, or rather it suddenly happens and permanently lasts. Applied to accepting our longings, this is the shift moment in which we hold these longings in our hearts without being so attached to having them fulfilled nor so angry at the partner who can't seem to satisfy them. The longings for the five A's then begin to stand alone rather than as justifiable only if they lead to fulfillment. We notice that we are feeling something existential, shared by all humans, rather than something unique to us. Compassion for ourselves and all humans may then awaken in us. A yes to our longings has led to a spiritual practice.

Like other animals, it is in our earliest relationships that we receive our most significant imprinting. From our experience in our family home, we form a concept about love. Then we are on the lookout for how future relationships match or do not match our model. This is the poignant origin of so many of our disappointments with others who do not measure up to a past they do not know. If our past was negative or hurtful, we may look for partner-candidates who will re-create that hurt, and then we can blame them, since perhaps we never fully felt or expressed our rage at a parent who wounded us that same way. This is how our demanding expectations are born, how our pent-up rage finally finds its chance to explode, how our hopes spring up or die.

Do We Hope or Despair?

If we missed out on one or all of the five A's, two possible results may occur, both painful: We might now need them in an extreme way. Our heart is then a bottomless pit, never getting enough. A second alternative is despair, not believing that the five A's of intimacy are there to be had, not trusting that anyone or anything can provide or foster them for very long. Such despair is deadly, since it finds no way to resolve itself. *How can I make despair a question rather than an answer?*

Hope, expectation, and despair reside in all of us. Whichever happened in childhood lingers on in us and then becomes activated in an intimate relationship. We then transfer onto others our hope that they will come through for us, our expectation that they will make up for all our past deficits, or our despair of them ever really being there for us. We can even *cause* any of these three options to happen:

In the transference based on *hope* we ask those we love, often tentatively and indirectly, to provide us with what was missing from our past. We believe others, some others, can indeed be trusted to be there for us. In the transference based on *expectation* we demand this. In the transference based on *despair* we anticipate and fear repetition of failures at attuning to our needs. We imagine that an adult partner will disappoint us as our parents did, and we shame ourselves for being unworthy or blame our partners for being ungiving.

The first and second may lead us to cling and the third may lead us to run. These oscillate as figure to ground in the course of an adult relationship. Hope helps us trust the givens of our lives as ingredients of growth and helps us to say yes to them no matter what they lead to, that is, unconditionally. Expectation may lead us to attempt to force others to give us what we need, directly or in passively aggressive ways. Despair may turn some basic forms of trust that most people have accepted into disturbing questions, never fully settled:

Does life have meaning?
Am I am worthy to live and be happy?
Does the universe have a loving intent?
Can women/men be trusted to help rather than hurt me?
Is growth and change truly possible?

Relationship is often a forced rerun characterized by a troubled hope that this time around it might be better for us. We transfer our original dashed expectation onto a new source of hope. In that sense, transference represents a touching fact about us. We have an irrepressible longing for love no matter how often we are let down. We keep hoping for better than we had. Alternatively, we may despair of anything improving for us, based on a long-standing negative template. We do all that it takes to make either—or both—of these come true in a new relationship.

Thus, we engage in transference because of our need for a repetition of the negative past or because of our hope for something new in the present. *Perhaps this time my needs will be greeted with fulfillment rather than disappointment.* We may live in hope for what will be better or we may fear what will be the same or worse. Sometimes both happen at once.

Is there a middle way between hope and despair? It is the unconditional yes to the given of life that our needs are sometimes met and sometimes not, that life is not always predictable, that things do not always come out the way we want. Between the extremes of hope and despair there flies a wise owl. He is the one that lands not in the marshes of wishful thinking nor in the desert of despondency but on the tree of life, the reality of how things are in the human world. We can sit with him on any branch of mindfulness. There we feel a sense of divine balance and we realize that our unconditional yes was how we aligned ourselves to it. Wallace Stevens expresses it in his poem *Notes Toward A Supreme Fiction:*

> *. . . not balances*
> *That we achieve, but balances that happen,*
> *As a man and a woman meet and love . . . .*

How Childhood Continues into Our Adult Relationships

In this section each paragraph gives a specific example of how transference moves from childhood into our adult lives and relationships.

If in childhood our household was full of tension, especially if one or both parents were addicted or psychologically impaired, the cells of our bodies might still hold some of the original level of anxiety. We might notice two possible results. We cannot feel fully comfortable except in an adrenaline-driven relationship, job, or lifestyle. Or we might be on red alert for danger and thus become so self-protective as to be closed off from others. These are examples of how transference burrows into our very cells, even though our minds report there is no danger now. Our minds know well, but our bodies know better.

Instant anger is often a sign of transference. For instance, in a childhood in which a boy's every move was scrutinized by his mother, his innate need for freedom of movement (the "A" of allowing that is often the dad's role to ensure) was ignored and he felt stifled. Now when he is comfortably in his office at home and his wife calls to him: "What are you doing in there?" he hits the ceiling—feeling again the sense of intrusion by a woman. If he has explored his past, he may recognize his extreme reaction as part of a displacement from childhood. If he has not, he will take his anger out on her and blame her rather than taking responsibility for the work he has to do on himself. The work is addressing, processing, resolving, and integrating his mother issue.

During my marriage, I recall occasionally, in my thoughts, confusing my wife with my mother. I also recall being unkind to my wife occasionally, even though she was kind to me. I wondered over the years why I was like that toward her. Recently, I was thinking of my ex-wife and again used the word *mom*. Suddenly I had my answer: I was getting back at mother for her harshness toward me in childhood through my wife, the new significant woman in my life. It was an important insight for me. I explained all this to my ex-wife, now a friend, and I apologized for my unconsciousness. I saw so clearly how transference can be dangerous to a relationship as long as it remains unconscious.

When a transference reaction becomes conscious, we may suddenly recall the exact nature of the original events of our past. For instance, when my sister continually criticizes me and I keep taking it, I may one day recall that this is precisely how my mother treated me. Then I may speak up, usually in anger, and that reaction will be directed at both the sister in front of me and the mother behind her. In another example, a man sees how his wife shows the five A's to her son and he is envious. Her affection is reminding him of what his own mother did not give him. The signal is envy; the work is grief for what he missed out on. Here is a final, more poignant example: From the way I love my son, I realize my father did not love me.

We were often blamed in childhood, so now we hear blame when others express healthy anger toward us. We feel criticized when others give us reasonable feedback. Even healthy anger directed at us by another feels scary when it is picking up on transferred energy. For instance, it may remind us of how father came at us so menacingly in childhood. The reminding can be conscious (our minds remember) or unconscious (our cells remember). Our fear of others' anger may keep us always on the alert, and we become adept at smoothing things over so that anger will not erupt. Such alertness is itself a form of pain.

A wife may act like a mother; a husband may act like a father. This is the equivalent of reliving our parent's life rather than becoming persons in our own right. Erotic passion for our partners fades quickly when we become parent figures. Is the transference then a way of avoiding intimacy?

Transference may explain why we overstay in relationships that do not work so well. We may be too hasty in blaming ourselves as needy or foolish. Perhaps we hang on because we are trying to work out a whole lifetime of issues and this one relationship seems so apt a stage on which to accomplish it. We stay because the dim and flaring lamps of our childhood still light the stage.

A distressed, unfulfilled past calls for grief work before it can be laid to rest. When we find a partner who seems to offer the fulfillment of all that we missed in childhood, we jump into his arms. He stands in as the parent who this time will come through for us. We thus hop over the grief requirement. Then grief becomes the missing link in our journey toward psychological health. Transference makes the missing link look like a bridge. This mistake is trickster energy, since it eventually shows us our skipped step rather than letting us skip it. We soon find all the same issues arising with a partner that we hoped to skip over from childhood. Under the bridge we constructed, our psyche was constructing its own bridge to export its shipment into our adult relationships. But, ah, the missing link of grieving turns out to be a required link between a wounded childhood and healthy adult intimacy.

Transference can happen because of a similarity between a parent's psychological type and a partner's. For instance, an introverted husband may trigger our impatience with our distant, introverted dad. We might be attracted to an introverted, unavailable person so that we can finally turn him—that is, dad—around.

Our parents had the power of life and death over us. We had to please them in order to survive in the earliest era of our existence. Now, when we transfer the parental imago onto someone, with the transference might come the same need to please. We give our power over to the other, since survival and likability seem to be identified, as they were in childhood. This is how our unconscious transference can prevent us from growing up.

We might notice transference when we idealize or demonize someone. In such primitive transference we are seeing a person in the larger-than-life size our powerful parents had in our childhood. In such mistaken identity we are apt to give away our power and serenity to the idealized other, who has become so necessary to our happiness, or the demonized other, who so strongly evinces our fear and our need to be on the defensive. Someday we may resent how much of our mental space was taken up by that one little person whom we so inflated. The stature of all our inner figures, like our own ego, has to be reduced to more appropriate dimensions if we are ever to be free.

Problems with authority take the form of automatic opposition or unquestioning obedience. We then find ourselves either unable to trust or overly trusting. Such reactions are often a sign of a parental transference. We are still enraged at the mother who was so controlling. We cannot trust the person who does that because he is attempting to override our deepest needs, values, and wishes—the core of who we are. A controlling father who insisted we meet his expectations engenders anger in a child, and that anger will later find a target at which to aim itself, such as a boss or any authority figure. Anger is specific to a person or circumstance, hence limited; rage is diffuse and without limits. It gathers momentum from long-standing insult and unfairness that has never been addressed or redressed. When we were pressured by our parents not to cry or to show anger or to be afraid, we might have come to believe that feelings could be controlled. That myth can explain our attempts—or our need—to be in control now.

We may notice that a certain touch, especially by a stranger, takes on greater meaning than fits the bill. This can be a clue that we may be so needy for a sense of acceptance that we make more of a touch than is meant by it. Perhaps in childhood we constructed our sense of ourselves from just such fleeting moments and now we transfer that power onto what happens in the present between us and others. But our sense of self was never meant to come from that quarter. What we feel may be a faux sense of self from a misinterpreted moment. Sadly, for some of us, even the sense of neediness sometimes stands in for a sense of self. Then we see a partner as a *source* of happiness rather than as a *context* that fosters it, the more adult version of relating to an intimate partner.

It will be tough to let go of the relationship, even when it does not work, if our identity has melded in with another person. *Could it be that one of the reasons it is so hard to let go is that so much of ourselves has been transferred onto others? This may account for our belief that we will not survive if we leave or lose a relationship.*

Transference also appears in our illusory belief in a bigger meaning than is appropriate to the signals we are getting. For instance, a severely withdrawn person may imagine that he has a girlfriend because the woman next door smiles at him as she passes him in the corridor. He is transferring onto her the expectations he developed from his mother's or schoolteacher's smile.

Transference is pathological when it becomes abusive or harmful to ourselves or others. For instance, a person who has been the victim of abuse in childhood may transfer his feelings of low self-worth onto someone else and become a persecutor. The original victim now feels in control (as he believes his own abuser was). This is a counterphobic reaction that makes the victim/persecutor feel he is redressing the wrong done to him. This kind of transference may be part of the personality of serial killers. Carroll Cole, for instance, murdered women he believed to be dissolute. In his childhood, his mother was promiscuous and would force him to watch her acting sexually with other men, then later she would beat him to intimidate him into not telling his father. Notice also how his sense of being in control as an adult was confirmed by retaliation, the wounded ego's favorite equalizer.

A male partner may have unresolved rage toward a mother who controlled or abused him. In adult life he may engage in the game of seduction and withdrawal. He invites a woman into his life and seems available for a committed relationship, but he keeps declaring his "doubts" and breaking up. Then he comes back and draws her in again, only to pull back soon after. What is going on? He is sincerely confused on the conscious level. Unconsciously, he is setting a scene of seduce-and-withdraw, a scene he may repeat often. When he seduces the woman in, he sees her come toward him with nurturing love. This love reminds him of mother's approach that became engulfing. Now, unlike in childhood, he can reject mother/women. The rejection of the woman in the present finally achieves a freedom from his smothering mother in the past. The wise woman will not go through this cycle of seduce-and-withhold more than once. The wise man will hightail it to therapy to work on a transference that has become a fear of and punishment of women. Of course, the roles can be reversed male to female also.

We may act kindly and want to be kind. Yet our unconscious may be mean in spite of our conscious intentions. We occasionally have mean thoughts or do things that are cruel. Both seem out of character, and we wonder, "Where did *that* come from?" It is as if some of our inner territories were never reached by the missionaries of loving-kindness, nor yet colonized by a civilized empire. For instance, we did not intend to be aggressive when we teased, tickled, or pinched our partner. Yet these are indeed aggressive, pain-producing acts. We are consciously playful, but our *hostile unconscious* has kicked in. This may be reminiscent of how our otherwise loving parents or siblings in childhood came at us in similar "friendly fire" ways.

We call Mother in New York and her first words are, "So you are finally calling me!" We feel judged and guilty. We react with apologies, but she continues to reprove us. Then we erupt into indignation, and an argument begins. Now the full scenario, so reminiscent of our past together, is being played out. We are still caught in a one-note relationship that misses out on the love that certainly exists between us but cannot peep out from under the double blankets of our guilt and her anger. Is the expression of that love what we have feared in one another for most of our lives? Do the guilt-tripping and resultant anger serve to keep us safe from ever being truly intimate with each other? Is this our game? An alternative to such stimulus-response behavior is simply to pause between them long enough to find a way to break the cycle. To pause is, admittedly, hard to do when we are so heated by that one and only still-so-powerful voice at the other end of the phone and of our lives. In any case, in this and in any altercation with a partner or family member, we can always end with our own silent loving-kindness practice: "May you and I love more authentically. May we both act from an enlightened place. May we/you be well and happy."

A final comment on the above example may help us explore one more angle of ourselves. Our childlike reaction to our mother shows that we have a psychological issue that is regressive, still caught in the past. Another example might be that of adult siblings who are still acting like rivals rather than accepting the given that parents will sometimes prefer one of their offspring over the other. We can ask ourselves how many of our issues are those of childhood and how many are truly adult? Not only are we meant to grow up, but our concerns are also. Once we say yes without stammer or stutter to how the past played out for us and truly let go of it, we make room for adult issues, such as building self-esteem, successful relationships, and spiritual consciousness. *Is this what we are trying to avoid when we don't let go of the past?*

Our present partner may serve as the most recent understudy for the original stars of our drama in childhood. We might ask, "What did my psyche see in her that made her so apt an actress for this role? Perhaps she was the most suitable scarecrow on which to hang the tattered rags of my past, rags of childhood promises believed but unkept." How ironic that we can use others in that way even though they have an integrity and personality all their own. It must be that transference is a technology of the psyche to recover its losses as Emily Dickinson says:

> The Shapes we buried, dwell about,
>   Familiar, in the Rooms—
> Untarnished by the Sepulcher,
>   The Moldering Playmate comes—
> In just the Jacket that he wore—
>   Long buttoned in the Mold
> Since we—old mornings—Children—played . . . .
> The Grave yields back her Robberies—
> The years our pilfered things . . . .

2

What Transference Does and Why

Time present and time past
Are both perhaps present in time future,
And time future contained in time past.
—T. S. Eliot, "Burnt Norton"

Much of our childhood may be unsayable, but it is not inexpressible, and transference lets the story be told in spite of our muteness. We act out what we cannot quite cry out. We locate those who shall stand in loco parentis: We unconsciously beg from our intimate partner what we were refused by our mother. The story of our deprivation has to be told before the gift of our love can be given. We hope the other will take the clue and make up for what we missed. When that happens, we feel truly loved. This is why we can give love in return most easily to those who understand us.

The muteness-turned-transference also takes the form of acting toward a partner as a significant person acted toward us so we can show what happened. For instance, we withhold intimacy from others, as we play the part of our own ungiving parent. We do this not because we are tight-fisted about giving our love but because we are compelled to let the world know how deprived we were in receiving love. Only when we get something like that off our chest can our heart be opened.

Likewise we may not be manipulating our partner because we are simply controllers. We are stammering out in actions rather than in words how invaded we felt by our father's harsh control of us. We are showing as a way of telling, using a metaphor instead of a statement. In fact, the Greek word for "transference" is our word *metaphor*. Our present relationships are metaphors for our original bonds, both successful and failed. Intimacy is the momentary liberation from metaphorical comparisons into reality beyond compare.

We show what happened to us rather than simply telling it. We are doing this not because we are playing it close to the vest or lying. The showing rather than telling happens because we are unconscious of the impact of the past and unconscious of the ways we are repeating it through transference.

The Clues

Transference is a code. A code is a full explanation of something but in a secret format that has to be broken into in order to be understood. Transference holds complex clues about the past, still waiting to be untangled. The ways we transfer onto others give us code names about what happened in the past. What we so frantically long for from a partner may be code for what we missed from a parent or former partner. What we expect from a relationship is code for what really happened on those distant days in our family kitchen or in the barn with our cousin or with our first spouse in our honeymoon cottage.

Since transference is unconscious, a clue to it is the sense that we know something but don't know how we know it. We have a sense of someone having power to seduce or repel us, but we cannot put our finger on exactly why. That "why" goes back many decades to our childhood, with its compelling drama of suspense and its cast of characters, mysterious at times, since we were not so sure of their roles: *Are they here to love or hurt me?* The adults in our childhood world were also mysterious to us because they were usually not as open about themselves as our friends were. So much of the day they were gone. Who knows where? So much of the time they were acting in ways that made no sense to us. Who knows why? So much of our knowledge of their motivations had holes that had to be filled in. Who knows how? So many secrets from their past were whispered so we could not hear. All of that became the puzzling "Why?" that plagues us now. Our fascination with solving whodunits is understandable, given how much of our own past was a mystery.

The most common clues to transference are the following: stronger feelings than seem to fit the circumstance, instant reactions, holding on to a relationship when it is not working, obsession, unexplainable attraction or repulsion, confusion about whys and wherefores, personalizing others' actions, and a similarity in the characteristics of all our partners. In addition, the way we describe our relationship may be an exact depiction of our childhood. For instance, "I am not really being noticed here" or "I can feel that my needs are being mostly met." Our words reveal a clue to what childhood was like and to how we have located precisely the relationship that recapitulates it.

Clues to transference definitely come to us in our reactions to films. We cry, laugh, or feel fear at certain moments and don't know why. We become engaged in a scene or character and can tell we are reacting more strongly than is accounted for by what is happening on the screen. We are relating to the characters and events as projections of our own story. We are finding out what we really felt in similar moments in our own lives and how we still feel even now. We are moved by the plight of the hero and we guess it is or was our own. We hear the heroine say just what we would have said if we had been free to do so. We see tears that we were meant to shed. We shed tears that were waiting their turn.

Our projections onto others are clues. It takes us a while to notice how much of who we are has been residing in others. Indeed, transference shows us that other people are not out there as totally other. They are reflections/projections of our own story. They are part of us. They are not only "they"—or "he/she"—but also "I." For instance, we see our ex-spouse and realize she no longer evokes the old magic to seduce and thrill us. No adrenaline rushes in, only matter-of-factness, mild hostility, or a warm friendliness. We see clearly in that moment that what she has become to us shows us that projection, transference, and displacement accounted for a great deal of the original exciting attraction/chemistry. The fervent sexual energy we called love felt so real fifteen years ago. Yet it seems impossible to recapture it now, nor do we have the slightest interest in doing so. The recognition of transference deepens our wonder about exactly how the relationship was real. How much of my significant other was constructed from my significant others?

We may find a clue to transference when we notice how we react exactly as one of our parents did, for instance, with sudden rage or storming off. Transferential feelings sometimes cross the generations in a forward direction. For instance, we see many of a former husband's traits in our son. We may then take some of our anger meant for husband out on son. Either physical or psychological resemblance can make for transference. Here is a positive example from a poem by Anne Bradstreet, "A Letter to Her Husband Absent upon Public Employment":

> *In this dead time, alas, what can I more*
> *Than view those fruits which through thy heart I bore . . .*
> *True living pictures of their father's face.*

Causes and Choices

Transference is a map of our life experience showing the territory we have covered and how we keep going back to it. Transference is thus recursive, that is, an effect goes back to a cause, which causes another effect. It is thereby a self-contained process. It is self-defeating if we do not catch this algorithm in the act and call it for what it is. We can then use it to confront our past's insidious interference in our present.

To work with transference takes attention to past causes of our present behavior. Causes issue from the vocabulary of reason and orderliness. However, there is another vocabulary we can access. It is that of *choices*. For instance, one theory is that criminals become soured on society because of the abuse they experienced in childhood. Another theory is that they are fully responsible no matter what happened to them in the past. Instead of an either-or approach, we can appreciate the impact of the past and see how it influences present behavior but does not excuse it. We combine cause and choice in looking at our psychological issues also. Transferential causes do not excuse, but they do influence, our choices. The work is to see the influence rather than let it remain unconscious. Then we can make new choices that reflect our adult responsibility.

Recursive transference also resembles the heroic journey by which our parents' role is to launch us into the world. Leaving home does not mean simply changing one's address. It does not mean breaking the deep connections we have with our families. That is not true individuation, since it contradicts the nature of being human. Leaving home is a metaphor for our growth into adulthood by blowing down the house of cards we have constructed from our complex story lines of who we are and what the world owes us. To leave such a nest of illusions is to find the courage to walk "as refugees in no-man's land," as Chögyam Trungpa, the Tibetan meditation master, put it. This is a land where nothing serves to confirm our ego's solidity or entitlements. To leave home is to leave an imagined safety from pain for an openness to the givens of life, which we greet with an unconditional yes. That word yes is our open sesame to waking up, our spiritual victory.

Yet, as the eighth-century Indian Buddhist teacher Shantideva reminds us, "We, like senseless children, shrink from suffering while we seek its causes." Most of us want to recover from the past and yet we keep repeating it. At the same time, our unconscious transference feelings are used to defend us against facing conflicts from childhood that are now revived in what seems to be a safer setting, an adult relationship, and with a presumably safer person, an intimate partner. We keep looking for nests when our freedom consists in leaving them for the open air.

In the unconscious, all is flow: there is no past and future separate from the present. Everything recapitulates what has gone before and is arched toward what is to come, in what David Bohm called a "holomovement." Likewise we experience reality not in discrete pieces but in quanta, collections of experience. Arthur Koestler, scientist and philosopher, taught that everything is a "holon," a whole that is part of another greater whole and yet is more than can be accounted for by its parts. Each part wants to endure as its autonomous self and participate in the purposes of the whole. Transference vividly demonstrates that every person is a holon, part of a greater story, always shown, not always told.

Noticing What We Are Up To

I know I am not seeing things as they are. I am seeing things as I am.
—Laurel Lee

Here are summary and further comments that help us understand
how transference works:

- We do not simply remember an event or loss mentally. We feel it,
  and this feeling is a signal that we have something to address, process,
  resolve, and then integrate. Instead, we might refer it to, transfer it
  onto someone else who resembles the characters in our story. In
  transference reactions, we repeat rather than remember. In this
  sense, our transference is a way of resisting the full implication of
  a memory. At the same time, when we catch ourselves at it, we can
  practice cutting through to the memory and the work it will take
  to deal with it. This is how becoming conscious of transference
  revives the past so that we can find a path into it and through it.
- Transference happens unconsciously, but this is not surreptitious
  on our part. It may be our way of protecting ourselves from direct
  contact with something from our past that we are not ready to realize. Secrets are indeed necessary in some areas of life, for example prayer, contemplation, sexual intimacies, creative works in
  progress. The secret of deep meaning may be hidden from us because it is too mysterious for minds like ours to plumb. As James
  Hillman writes, "Resistance and secrecy are based upon the unknown and unknowable at the core of psychic life."
- Transference is sometimes difficult to distinguish from ordinary
  relationship needs. This is because our earliest needs—attention,
  acceptance, appreciation, affection, and allowing, for instance—
  turn out to be the same needs we have in an intimate relationship.
  Transference comes in as an unconscious throwback to our original story and how it played out. Instead of simply seeking need-
  fulfillment in an adult way, we add on expectations and entitlements
  that belong more legitimately to the parent-child relationship.
- The term *transference resistance* refers to our failure to recognize
  transference when it is pointed out to us. We can also use transference to avoid the anxiety of knowing about our past, because it
  would be too overwhelming to face. We can use transference in
  a relationship to hold back on experiencing real intimacy with a
  real person. We might do this either because we fear that level of
  closeness or are not yet fully trusting of the other.

- Our transferences influence, or even at times determine, how we see others. Most of us come to relationships with preformed opinions. We use our own peculiar dictionary of meanings and myths as we walk out onto the human stage. These play out as demands, yearnings, and expectations, and become the raw material of transference. Our longing to receive the five A's of childhood from adult relationships is not foolish but touching and revealing of the punctures in our past. Our useful itch for wholeness emerges from our sense of limitation. It is only because something is missing that we reach out for what transcends ego. In this sense, our limitations are not inimical to our growth. The holes in us are assisting forces on our journey toward personal fulfillment. The work is to identify our gaps so we can work on them. Then we are more likely to join Thoreau in saying to a partner, "I will come to you, my friend, when I no longer need you. Then you will find a palace, not an almshouse."
- Words have a denotation, the dictionary meaning, and a connotation, that which is suggested or evoked. For instance, the denotation of *mother* is a female biological parent, but that word evinces immediate feelings and reactions in us based on what it connotes. This connotation is both personal, based on our history with our own mother, and collective, based on our universal human sense of what is in the universal mother archetype. Transference is connotation.
- Transference is not a problem but an acting out of an abiding—and legitimate—continuity between the present and the past. Yet, we cannot forget that the past as it happened historically is not necessarily the same as the past we carry unconsciously. We are memory banks that do not necessarily keep accurate track of our accounts.
- The term *transference* is also used medically to refer to the process by which a symptom is relocated in another part of the body. This is a metaphor for what happens in psychological transference in that we often relocate our pain rather than remove it. For instance, we find new ways to feel the desolation of childhood by staying in a relationship with someone who is unfaithful. We appear to the outside world to be "the faithful one" but in reality we are the orphaned one, again. An orphan is anyone who did not receive or is not receiving the five A's.

- The line of development of a transference is autonomous. Our intellectual development does not necessarily match or track with our psychological development. Transference happens no matter how smart we are, no matter how careful or how healthy. Transference is a deep structure of human relationships, that is, an essential feature, universally present.
- Transference happens because humans relate in rhythmic, flowing ways, give and take, back and forth, event and repetition. Even without issues with our parents, we would displace, project, and transfer, since we are beings who easily slip out of the smart embrace of present reality into the enchanting grip of the imaginary world. We do not want to lose the creativity in our imaginations, only stop enticing others into joining our rogue theater company.
- Transference happens because we humans naturally use symbolization to process our experience. A simple example is in how we tell a friend or therapist of a traumatic event. We use metaphors and gestures that symbolize our experience, and thereby we find help in working it through. In transference a person here and now symbolizes someone from the past with whom we have unfinished business. Symbolization can take one of two directions. It can lead to confusion if it remains unconscious. But when it becomes conscious and we do the work it points us to, it is transformative.
- To stop engaging in transference totally is like trying to kill off the unconscious. The goal is to notice and learn from transference, to reduce its wallop, to weaken its hold on our relationships, and to work on repairing what it reveals as damaged. In addition, since "father" and "mother" are archetypes in our collective unconscious, they can never be eradicated, nor should they be. In this regard we can note that Freud at first configured transference as a neurosis and a hindrance because it distorted the rapport between patient and therapist. Later, he came to see that transference is a fast track into accessing the unconscious. He also saw that a positive transference onto the analyst could assist in the patient's progress, since the kindly therapist could play the role of a new, more understanding father or mother and thereby help the client work through her emotionally unfinished business, safely at last.
- Transference is a valuable gift. It is a perfect record of what child-

hood was really like, what the transactions were about, what was really going on, what heaven was found or wished for, what hell we were condemned to or from which we escaped just in time. Transference is a recording of our childhood and our parenting, shouting out just how we felt. Awareness of transference is the opportunity to work on ourselves at last: to address, process, resolve, and integrate some of the seemingly lost and darksome past. We will explore this practice at the end of this chapter.

- Transference can have a satisfactory end. A transference-rich relationship provides crucial information about the deficits that may have characterized our primal relationship. We see how we still have an opportunity to grow out of it when we experience a revival of it. Self-psychologist Heinz Kohut's first definition of transference fits here: "Transference is a repetitive tendency of a repressed infantile drive attached to old objects that now seeks new objects in its search for satisfaction." Psychiatrist and writer Paul Ornstein adds, "Transference reactivates the thwarted need to grow." In this context, transference can also be about how we wished it would have been.

- Our psychological purpose in life is self-expression within and through human connections. As long as our relationships are unconscious re-treads of the past, we are not engaged in self-expression but in self-concealment. A healthy ego organizes a purposive self-expression toward others and toward the world. This cannot happen when we are relating to ideational representations of our past. We then become unable to deal with our past directly and consciously. Instead we slam it all into the closet of repression and keep enlisting cunning accomplices to keep it closed. They are the people we love or hate, or both, and never know why.

- A "field" in science is an area of influence, a force field that upholds the space-time continuum. Some fields change in time to fit new needs. The boundaries of a force field are porous, indefinite in extent. Transference is just such a borderless field in human psychology. Indeed, each of us is a field of energy with physical and spiritual extensions without boundary. We only seem like discrete beings with a certain height and weight and a name all our own. In reality we are not islands but inlets.

- Freud realized that transference is a form of *suggestibility*, like that which makes it possible to be hypnotized. Both transference and hypnotism are about submission to a superior power. Submission may be appealing in transference, since it is associated with the sense of safety: "As long as I submit and remain a child, I do not have to face disappointment or threat, since I am protected." Alfred Adler described the submission element in transference as an attempt to divest ourselves of our own power and place it in the hands of another.

- Transference may induce a series of improvisations. For instance, if I say, "Why are you hurting me?" this may lead you to believe you *are* hurting me. I might then entreat you, "Take care of me and be kind to me," and you might say, "I will be your parent." We improvise a chain of dramatic dialogue based on one original experience. The chain can be forged internally too: "Why didn't you get here earlier?" asked by a friend may lead us to infer, "I am disappointing to him and not adequate," a reaction transferred from childhood judgments about us.

- In many religious traditions the role of the teacher is important. That relationship, even within careful limits, is not free of transference. We might see a kindly or stern father or mother in a teacher. In mature spiritual consciousness, such a transference does not have to interfere with the teachings being transmitted. For adults, the teachings are the teacher.

- Transference, like life itself, reaches us across the generations. Our ways of relating are not only based on our life with our parents. We were seeing them play out issues and myths they brought into our lives from their parents. Who knows how far back their fear of touching us may go? Who knows how long ago the family trait began of which we are now the unwitting heirs? The sense of continuity across the decades is also reflected in religious and civic life. Successive conservators maintain beliefs and traditions. We see this, for example, in respect for the U.S. Constitution in civic life, in transmission of the dharma from enlightened masters, or in handing on the Gospel message in apostolic succession.

- Past events feel present in a trenchant way when they first arise from repression. This makes our transferences seem like authentic transactions. We need not rebuke ourselves for missing the point. Therapy may help us make sense of it all.

- Transference is a universal habit of the unconscious, so it is quite appropriate in therapy since its focus is on the unconscious. How sad that sophisticated consciousness is such a petite and delicate component of a psyche that is mostly primitive. As the scientist Tim Ferris rightly remarks, "Consciousness is like a campfire in the middle of a dark Australia."

- Transference shows us the difference between conscious and unconscious factors in our decisions and choices. When our childhood experience was disappointing or inadequate in fulfilling our needs and we meet someone we find appealing or with whom we feel a chemistry, our motivation may either be exactly what we see it as or it may be twofold:

Consciously, I Believe That This Person Will:	*Unconsciously, I Found a Person Who Will:*
Help me repair my past experience	Repeat my past experience
Create the opposite experience of my past	Re-create my original experience
Replace someone from my past with a lively alternative	Duplicate someone from my past with a dead ringer
Provide me all that I missed out on in the past (a blind alley in which I seek to avoid my work on my past)	Take me into what was unhealthy in my past so I can at last deal with it by seeing it played out, recalling how it felt, mourning it, and letting it go (a path to healthy relating now)
Give me a fast track to healing	Confront me with the work I need to do

We Have Good Reasons to Transfer

It is an old southern-Italian custom not to begin eating dinner until all the family members are assembled around the table. The father does not allow the meal to get under way until every adult and child is in his or her proper place. This can serve as a metaphor for transference. It seems that we cannot proceed with life comfortably until our family issues are complete, everything on the table, and everyone in his place around it. This may help us understand why we engage in transference. By our transferences we reassemble our family around us, each member in his proper place, using just the right characters to take their places around us in the present. Unconsciously, we believe that once that happens, and perhaps only when and because that happens, we can truly nourish ourselves and get on with our life contentedly.

We have noticed positive reasons for transference in our earlier pages. Here are the ten central positive reasons that we engage in transference:

1. We are attempting to gain closure on issues that are backlogged and we cannot easily work them out with the original characters in our story. The person on whom we transfer is a catalyst for working through our old issues.

   We are trying so desperately to get the story out in every detail, a story not even we know fully. Transference helps us ring down the curtain on our past. Once we make our transference conscious, we have found a way of growing up, of growing past our family stuck places, and of healing our wounds.

   James Hillman writes, "One finds oneself inside a myth, which is neither true nor false, but simply the precondition for fitting one into the family drama as a recognizable character." Our life is a family theater, and transference is how the play is staged.

   What is left over finds a way of being worked out in the three-step transference cycle: *unconscious displacement of feelings* becomes *conscious recognition of what is incomplete* and that leads to *working on completing it.*

2. By means of transference, early on, we seek out those who will pinch-hit for the needs our parents failed to step up to the plate for. For instance, our teachers in grade school often fulfilled a nurturant parental role. Without transference all need-fulfillment would depend on those two little people, our parents. Transference

is a resource that makes parents, so limited, less crucial to our development. In healthy transference we expand the playing field. The whole village provides parenting, as was meant to happen in nature's plan. Transference serves what the extended family served for past generations—though even then transference was happening.

3. The ego is not immutable but continually changing and evolving. Thus, being true to oneself means living in accord with our ever-evolving deepest needs, values, and wishes. Their significance began in childhood. An active useful life can drown out our real needs, so we go on for years not knowing that something important is missing. Transference makes it possible to continue recognizing our original needs and seeking their fulfillment in age-appropriate ways, the essence of personal development. This is a creative venture on our part, and transference can be one of the artistic instruments we make use of: "The small boy [in me] is still around and possesses a creative life that I lack," wrote Carl Jung.

4. In an alcoholic home, we might not have known which mother would greet us when we got home from school. Would it be the kind sober mother or the drunken, abusive, or needy mother? We would design our role in the house in accord with how much vodka was left in the bottle. Our home was not then a safe holding vessel but a frightening cauldron in which a false and intimated self had to be devised if we were not to drown. We had to hide something about ourselves in order to preserve it. We go through life believing that finding out who we really are will devastate us. But information does not hurt us, it only builds a platform from which we can leap into growth.

We were born with an evolutionary expectation of being cared for. The lack of what was instinctively known to be so necessary, namely a safe home that provided the five A's, remains in us as a sense of discrepancy. We feel our childhood deficit ever after, something missing, something meant to come to us that never fully arrived, something longed for that even now is not quite fulfilled. We then emerge from childhood as Emily Dickinson did:

A mourner walked among the children . . .
I went . . . as one bemoaning a dominion . . .
Still softly searching for my delinquent palaces . . . .

We seek need-fulfillment in all the wrong palaces. This is how we impoverish ourselves. When we look for the wrong things, we get less.

5. When they are consciously engaged in, transference and counter-transference can be forms of compassion by providing motherly, fatherly, brotherly, or sisterly moments to one another. In Buddhism we hear the recommendation that we treat all beings well, since they were our parents in past lives. Perhaps that statement can be applied to our partners in this life, who keep bringing our parents back to life for us.

6. Much of childhood is lost or blurred in our memory. Transference opens windows into what our household was like. We can actually reconstruct our past by examining what we think, say, feel, expect, believe, and do in an intimate relationship now. We are probably acting like one of our parents or treating our partner as we were treated by our parents or training our partner to treat us as our parents treated us. Transference shows us where the bodies are. Then we can bury the dead and live with the living.

7. Transference makes it possible for us to gain from a stage or film drama in that we thereby experience a catharsis of our own conflicts and feelings through those of the actors. "Dramatic irony" refers to the moment in a play when a character with limited knowledge faces something that has much more power or meaning than he imagines. Transference is just such dramatic irony. What looks to us like a predicament of the actors we see on stage or in film is weighty with significances from our own life. In a play, the actors leave the stage when their role is finished. In transference, each actor hangs around backstage waiting for just the right cue so he can get back on stage and continue to play his role in up-to-the-minute words and newly designed costumes.

Likewise, most of us never see the truly dark behaviors humans engage in. Nor do we guess our potential for heroic love. Films and plays show us the full spectrum of human hate and love. Thus our reactions to them tell us something about our own positive and negative hidden qualities, our shadow, as well as our own transferences.

8. Transference combines illusion and truth. It is illusory since it confounds time sequences and people. It is real since it acknowledges that the present does indeed contain the past and that some people really do resemble other people. In this sense, transference is a paradox, always a clue to depth and spiritual meaning. The depth happens because we are seeing behind and through surfaces to what is hidden from superficial view. Thus, we see through the moment into the past. We see through this person to another more significant person. The spiritual dimension of transference is in the combination of apparent opposites as one.

   The legacy of self-knowledge from the human family has followed a three-phase path over the centuries. The first pathway was myth. Then religion held the vocabulary and rituals of our evolution. Finally, depth psychology brings us soul information. All three are still necessary if we are to experience the riches of human-divine wisdom.

9. The transference experience can be cosmic/collective, not simply personal. *Collective* means "not confined to any particular individual but applicable to and characteristic of all people." For instance, throughout history people have shown *bhakti* (devotion) to a mother goddess. Since nurturant mothers are so necessary to our growth, we may have found in the Virgin Mary, Kuan Yin, or any divinity or saint an unconditionally giving female archetype that supplemented the inadequacies of our own mothers. Transference makes religious devotion possible and helps grant access both to its comforts and its incentives to virtuous living. We will discuss this aspect of transference in greater detail in a later chapter.

10. Finally, we can gain from the fact that other people transfer onto us. They help us become recognizable to ourselves. We learn how we appear to others and which archetype we represent by our behavior. Our strong reactions to how others see or treat us does not have to lead to an ego defensiveness. We can be taught and healed by our arousal:

The trilling wire in the blood
Sings below inveterate scars
And reconciles forgotten wars.
—T. S. Eliot

Practice
Address, Process, Resolve, and Integrate

This is the first of many practices in this book. Our practices are not intended as ways of hammering on or chiseling away at ourselves. They are not aggressive. We are not trying to root out something but rather to open someone. In the old model, the accent in taming wild horses was to "break" the horse, to wear him down, show him who is boss, break his spirit. Now the accent is on "joining with" the horse. The trainer uses a cooperative, not a domination, model. Our practices are in that realm. We are taming our ego gradually and without force, but nonetheless definitely.

We put effort and discipline into our practices. We deepen our work when we acknowledge our need for help from assisting forces, transcendent powers that exist beyond our ego and help us go beyond our ego. We can begin each practice in this book with an aspiration to a higher power, in whatever way fits for us. We can ask for help while we practice and then offer thanks when a practice is complete. All of this acknowledges the role of grace in our progress and can move our psychologically oriented steps into spiritually healing shifts.

The heart of any psychological work is addressing, processing, resolving, and integrating the issue at hand. These words form the acronym APRI, which in Italian means "you open." As we understand this central and necessary four-part plan to complete our unfinished business, transference may not have to kick in so fiercely anymore.

We *address* the problem when we call it by name. We admit to ourselves what is really going on and our part in it, that is, we own our behavior and feelings. In addition, we are willing to look at our wounds and how we may have wounded others. We see our issue in a friendly way rather than critically. Thereby we coax it to reveal more about itself. This means staring into an experience rather than attempting to fix it quickly, rushing past it, glossing over it, or minimizing its impact. For instance, we admit that we have a drinking problem or a problem with anger. We acknowledge that our partner does not excite us because we are actually attracted to people of our own gender. We put our cards on the table. We let the truth come out and remain open to feelings in ourselves and others. When a child has been locked in a closet, he will come out angry. Revelation about a truth or freedom to move releases the lively energy of feelings.

We may notice two ways of addressing an issue with someone. We can size up what someone has done or said with a kind-hearted, sophisticated response or we can do the same thing with a primitive retort. Someone seems pushy; we can see that as missionary zeal and compulsion and can feel compassion without, nonetheless, letting that person control us. Or we can see it as persecutory and aggressive and want to judge and punish the other. In childhood we reacted to life and events mostly at a primitive level. That may still be our style, one that leads to judgment rather than focused addressing. As adults we can practice socializing and spiritualizing our ways of perceiving. Then we see with loving-kindness while not letting the wool be pulled over our eyes.

When our partner refuses to address an issue that affects our relationship, we are being given information that we might not want to face. We might say, "I need this to change," or "I hope this will change." If the issue is recent, those statements can help us mobilize toward working on a change. If the issues are long-standing and nonnegotiable, these statements can be evasions and self-appeasements. For instance, a spouse who has refused to have sex for years and refuses to discuss it or go to therapy has already made her statement. For us to address the issue means getting the message and asking, "Now what for me?" not "Maybe it will change." It is important to notice when transactions are over and personal action is the suitable alternative. As we become more courageous, getting on with life becomes more valuable than the narcotic comforts of the status quo.

Addressing, processing, resolving, and integrating are responses to issues in relationships. Divorce is defined in the dictionary as the official ending of a marriage by complete separation. Divorced people have implicitly agreed to end their emotional transactions, though child-caring or financial transactions may continue. Once we no longer engage emotionally with someone, as a divorce is meant to signify, there is no need to process feelings together. Some partners want to bring up the past and reopen sensitive issues after a divorce is final. There is no obligation to respond by addressing, processing, resolving, and integrating in that instance. The transactions have ended even though emotions may still be lively. An exception happens when old resentments are getting in the way of appropriate child care or financial settlements. Otherwise, the issue of the still-emotional partner is the province of individual therapy.

When two people have an issue between them, each person's unique timing certainly has to be respected. One person may be ready to deal with an issue while the other needs more time. At the far opposite ends of the healthy spectrum of timing is compulsion to face and finish something and procrastination. Couples and friends can come to terms with these differences by together addressing the issue of timing before they begin to tackle the issue itself.

To *process* is to express the feelings associated with the experience we are working on. We do this nonaggressively, not losing control. We take responsibility for our own emotions without blaming others. We may then see the hookup of our experience with something in our past, and our feelings do double duty as we feel for both the past and the present. Processing also includes looking at what we have been getting out of our predicament or feelings. For instance, we might feel angry in a relationship and be using that anger for its secondary gain to us, that of avoiding intimacy.

Such feeling and consciousness lead to *resolving*, which includes taking action. A resolution happens as a healing shift, a grace that comes into play. We do not make it happen; it simply results, because addressing and processing lead to dissolving of the problem. In this alchemical process, our expression of feelings leads to the evaporation of them and of all the unfinished business behind them. We resolve actively when we take the steps that lead to change. We join a twelve-step program if addiction is our issue. We break the old cycle and find new ways of behaving and new ways of seeing life and relationships. Resolving a problem in a relationship entails making agreements and keeping them.

To *integrate* our experience means reshaping our lives in accord with what we have gained and learned from addressing, processing, and resolving. We *implement* what we have worked on. This is consistency between what we have worked on and how we live our lives. We now live

and relate differently than before. Our choices were based on unconscious issues; now these issues have come to light. A light shining on our
world makes it look new, and we are free to live in accord with our true
deepest needs, values, and wishes. To use an analogy, our kitchen experience is automatically different when we use a sink rather than a pump,
or a dishwasher rather than a sink. Everything changes when an upgrade
occurs. *Was this what we feared all along?*

We can restate this in brief this way: *Addressing* leads to a release of
energy in the form of feelings. *Processing* these feelings leads to a shift so
that they finally evaporate. Processing also leads us to *resolve* things by
making agreements to bring about changes. This resolution leads to letting conflicts become matter-of-fact rather than ego-invested. Then we
redesign our lives to match our newfound changes. This is *integrating.*

We notice that each of the four steps is a *pause.* To address is to pause
to contemplate the fact, impact, meaning, and inner workings of an experience. To process is to pause long enough to feel all that goes with the
experience and to explore its connection to past patterns. We resolve for
the future to pause between a stimulus and our usual immediate reaction. This pause is freedom. We pause several times in every day that follows so that we can integrate what we have learned.

We might not go the route of the four steps. Instead, we might resist
completions, preferring the familiar behavior of repetition. Then that
resistance becomes the issue to address, and we can go through our same
four steps. They really work, and they help us trust ourselves as able to
handle what life and relationships toss our way. Our "Oh no, I can't face
or deal with that!" becomes "I can do this."

———————

The above practice may not work in a relationship with an addict, someone *trying to keep issues incomplete,* which is one of his forms of escape. We
can't expect otherwise until he finds a program of recovery. We are left
hanging, a given of relating to someone with that sickness. An Al-Anon
or equivalent program provides the best resources to help us move on.

The preceding fourfold plan may not be a truly skillful means if it is
rushed to the scene of our wounding so that we can "get over it" quickly.
Some events teach us so much when we allow them to work themselves

out in their own time and way. Some experiences have to be lived with for a while before they can resolve themselves. Time is required between problem and solution, question and answer, issue and resolution. We grow from resting in the ambiguity of that between-space. We gain an opportunity to feel our feelings all the way and to recognize our projections and transferences quite profoundly.

In the meantime, we may find our ego becoming destabilized, but that can be a path to a firmer sense of our adult powers. We can become stronger for the next time something challenges us in a similar way. Pausing respectfully in our confused ego state becomes a form of Buddhist *tantra,* the practice of using what is most negative and neurotic to find enlightenment. The between-pause can expand us, balance us, deepen us. Those three benefits are more valuable than the remedy we locate when we address immediately, process too swiftly, resolve too suddenly, and integrate prematurely. The compulsion to clear things up too facilely does not honor the timing all things take and may lose us the gift that time can give. As we mature in spiritual consciousness, we act more like farmers tending their crops than like generals ordering their troops.

Timing is an essential ingredient of transformation: A persimmon, when it first appears on the tree, is astringent. With time to ripen, it becomes sweet. As we honor the timing of events and people, even our questions soften and change. We no longer ask, "What has he or she done to me?" but "What can this be for me?" We do not ask, "Why did this happen to me?" but "How has this helped me grow?" In fact, every "Why?" becomes "Yes, now what?"

> *When unresolved issues are writing our life story, we are not our own autobiographers; we are merely recorders of how the past continues, often without our awareness, to intrude upon our present experience and shape our future directions.*
>
> —Daniel Siegel, MD

3

Ways We Can Be Together

Add love . . .
Then wilt thou not be loath
To leave this paradise, but shall possess
A paradise within thee, happier far.
—Milton, *Paradise Lost*

Though transference is happening in our relationships and interactions, it is not all that is happening. We humans intermingle in countless ways. There are three basic ways of relating that stand out. Each of them affects how we communicate:

1. *Matter-of-fact, straightforward* transactions are neutral, reality-based, and happen entirely in the present. Here we communicate as givers and receivers of information. "Matter-of-fact" does not mean cold/unfeeling but acting in accord with what something is in its pure state, before we began editorializing.
2. *Transference* is memory-based and is directed by the past. Here we communicate as actors and reactors to former losses, fulfillments, and expectations.
3. A *you-and-I* (also called I-thou) relationship is intimacy-based and happens in the unedited present. Here we communicate as participants in each other's experience, as truly present to each

other, collaborators in the practices of love. Ego-centeredness perpetuates separateness. The you-and-I relationship is co-presence,
described by Emily Dickinson in her poem "They put Us far
apart":

> *"I see thee" each responded straight . . .*
> *Each other's Face—was all the Disc*
> *Each other . . . saw.*

A simple way to tell which of the three levels is happening in any given
moment is to distinguish their various effects:

> Level 1. *Matter-of-fact transactions* simply inform us. There
> is no surge in our emotional circuits, though there may certainly
> be a sensation or feeling. The bond is real, but not impinging or
> strongly impactful. We do not engage in projection, but rather
> experience something or someone simply, straightforwardly,
> purely.
>
> Level 2. *Transference relationships* affect us. We act or react
> with strong feeling, and usually with adrenaline that indicates an
> ego ignited by fear or compulsive grasping. The bond is one of
> attachment or repulsion. We join into what we project and make
> it more than it is in its simplest truth. Sometimes transference is
> so strong that very little of the true other comes through to us.
> Then we have not an I-to-you but an I-to-me, the me being my
> collection of projections/assumptions and transferences that
> seem to be you!
>
> Level 3. *You-and-I intimacy* connects us. We give and receive
> warmth and holding that leads to mutual understanding. The
> bond is one of commitment. We engage with what we meet up
> with in reality rather than with what we might project onto it. If
> we are angry, our anger does not take the form of blaming oppo-
> sition but of communication of a feeling that easily coexists with
> love. The connection remains unbroken.

You-and-I is an event of immediate presence. This is an encounter
not only between two people. It is how we encounter *the between*—that

is, the soul-place where personality opens. Our personality is not in us but is a happening between us and those who attune to us. The between is thus the holding environment where authentic intimacy can occur. The word *soul* refers to the realm of the between, that is, between conscious and unconscious, past and present, time and eternity. A soul mate is one who bridges these with us, as the metaphor of a guardian angel shows and promises.

Here is an example of all three levels at work:

I am in the bank at the teller window, but I have not filled out my deposit slip. The unfazed teller takes my omission in stride and gives me an opportunity to fill it out there and then with no comment. I do so with no apology. This is level 1, a matter-of-fact, straightforward relating on both our parts. No energy is evinced during the event or after in either person.

If, on the other hand, a testy teller rebukes me, "Sir, you are required to fill out your forms before approaching the counter. There is even a sign saying that, right over there." Now I feel criticized and shamed. If this is reminiscent of how I was treated in childhood, I take what the teller said at level 2, transferring my father's face onto her and feeling instant rage. My ego will tell me I am justified in feeling abused and that it is the teller's fault that I feel as I do. The neurotic ego is the part of us that defends us in ways like that. This energy will stick in my craw and may keep gnawing at me later in the day. The alternative would have been to listen without being provoked into a strong feeling reaction and say, "Thank you, and I will pay more attention next time." Then I would have reduced the level from 2 to 1.

If however, as a third option, a kindly teller smiles, makes eye contact, and fills out the deposit slip for me with a comment like, "That's OK, many people forget and it's no big deal," I might thank her matter-of-factly. Or I might feel cared about the way I did by my always forgiving and helpful aunt. Positive transference occurs in that moment, and I might even think of that teller later or find her attractive. *How much of our attraction to others, especially in a first meeting, is a spin-off of transference?*

The matter-of-fact level is conscious. The transference level is unconscious, until we notice it and make the connection between what is happening in the present and how it recapitulates something from our past. You-and-I relating happens in a deep, intimate bond and is richly deliberate, a choice to see the other and be with her just as she is. The first two happen without effort; this third option takes intentional awareness, even practice.

We might also engage in a matter-of-fact relationship that is not neutral and still does impact us. Yet, it does not contain transference. *With some people there is no transference,* yet honest feelings happen and the interactions are important as well as memorable. Friends and colleagues are often in this category.

When there are strong feelings of attraction in our transference reactions, we might seek to upgrade the interaction to a level 3, a you-and-I relationship. When our chosen one instead insists on interacting only at the matter-of-fact level, we feel rejected and we might become angry or sad. A relationship can evolve healthily when we mutually move from level 1 to level 2 to level 3.

Two people may meet at the matter-of-fact level and either nothing more happens or some gesture leads to a transference reaction. This creates an interest that then blossoms into a relationship. Once they work through the transferences both may be carrying toward each other, they meet only as who they really are. Then the dramatic relating becomes the meeting of two unique individuals, free of projections. This is the culmination of intimacy. It is a rare relationship that does not ignite by transference. It is a wonderful accomplishment when the fire of love eventually burns away the transference so that only heart speaks to heart and a true I-thou blooms.

Communication problems occur in relationships when one partner means to express something at the matter-of-fact level and the other receives it at the transference level. What makes a divorce mean-spirited may be that the couple is still enmeshed in transference issues when it is time to become matter-of-fact. Only after they become matter-of-fact in their relating with each other can they act sensibly and kindheartedly. Then, eventually, a you-and-I can happen between them and they can meet as friends. A parent's face is gone and with it all the adrenaline that has mesmerized them during so many years of discord. Freedom from transference is often an entry into true acceptance of the other. How sadly ironic it is that we sometimes have to break up before we can be friends.

These same three levels of relating apply to a bond with the divine. We may believe intellectually that there is a God but make no attempt to relate to God personally nor design our life in accord with moral principles.

That is a matter-of-fact or superficial faith. We can imagine God as an extension of the father we had or wish we had, granting rewards or imposing punishments, blessing and protecting us if we obey him. This is a transferential faith. The experience of a relationship to God in a you-and-I communion through devotion and the practice of virtues is a living faith. We will explore all this more in detail in a later chapter.

Because of our unconscious transferences, only in rare, unguarded moments are we in an authentic you-and-I relationship. This is the moment in which we see the other exactly as he is and he sees us exactly as we are. Until a woman is free of mother or father meaning, she is not yet real to us. Until a man is free of father or mother meaning, he is not yet real to us. Until everyone is only who he is, be it God or human persons, we are not in full relationship. This is because the first task of development, to separate from our parents, has not yet happened. As long as we need to find others to play their parts in our lives, we have not yet left home.

The Real You, the Real Me

Alfred North Whitehead proposed that the world is composed of a series of innumerable bursts of momentary, discontinuous activity. He calls each moment an "actual occasion." Perhaps a you-and-I experience is just such an "actual occasion," like all the other realities in the universe.

In our transference onto someone, the other person is a holder of our history, our unconscious. A true you-I moment is one in which transference and projection vanish and all we see is the real person. This happens in the moments in which we are present with the five A's: We are attentively, acceptingly, affectionately, and appreciatively present to the other, allowing her to be who she is in that moment rather than making any attempts to control her. We are open to perceiving her for who she is, what she is saying, and what she is feeling. This is how someone feels truly loved by us.

In such moments—and they usually are only moments—we are unguarded, because in them we let go of our past long enough to be here now. Love unfolds best between two real people who greet each other with no phantoms from either one's past crouching in the room. Only then is there space for intimacy.

Such present-moment love restores, repairs, and rebuilds the inner world of our psyche, perhaps long ago misshapen or damaged. Then, through a combination of our work on ourselves and the confirming love others give us, a coherent sense of ourselves and an esteem for ourselves can emerge, however slowly or shyly. This increase in awareness and self-definition makes it possible to return love to others in the same confirming way. The beautiful paradox is that we receive and thereby learn to give. This is another example of the trustworthy economy of intimacy. We do not have to learn anything new, only renew. We do not have to give anything new, only give back.

In a true you-and-I relationship we are present mindfully, nonintrusively, the way we are present with things in nature. We do not tell a birch tree it should be more like an elm. We face it with no agenda, only an appreciation that becomes participation: "I love looking at this birch" becomes "I am this birch" and then "I and this birch are opening to a mystery that transcends and holds us both." In such moments, the ego has no wish for self-aggrandizement or domination. It is no longer triggered by transferences nor guarded by defenses. Instead, there is an engagement of individual liberties in a single unity.

How do we contact others just as they are without letting our own portraiture get in the way? It is the mindful presence that happens with the five A's and without ego mind-sets—fear, desire, judgment, interpretation, control, fantasy. This quality of presence frees us from dividing people into categories or pigeonholes. Then we can know and love others with mindfulness. Perhaps mindfulness is not only a practice but something we want to receive.

We cannot eliminate mind-sets, since they are natural to the mind, but we can place them in brackets rather than make them the subjects and predicates of our inner life. We do this when we notice and label our mind-set reactions rather than act on them. Mindfulness meditation is the practice that helps us do this.

In a relationship, we can sit mindfully with a problem and shave off mind-sets to see what it is really about: "What is this issue with my partner without the layers of fear, judgment, the need to fix or control, my illusions about it, my transferences around it?"

Mind-sets are the habits of the conceptual mind. Mindfulness undermines the mind-sets and thus frees us from dualism, because it endorses only the here and now as real. There is no interference from the mind-set of a fear of "there" or a wish for "elsewhere." There is no distraction by past or future, the fuels of transferences. There is only now. Practicing loving-kindness frees us from any remaining sense of separateness. This is how our spiritual work makes us more adept at relating in projection-free ways, and therefore more loving. *Can I stand your full-on presence, or will I keep hiding behind my transferences?*

The true self waits for just the right conditions before it can reveal its unconditioned identity. We all wait for the one who can say, "I am only I, and you are only you, and that is quite wonderful." This nurturant and yet entirely momentary you-and-I contains such a poignant irony: what we need from each other most is most ephemeral, evanescent. Yet no one is to blame. Momentariness is a given of every you-and-I relationship that is truly evolving.

Shakespeare alludes to the irony of our condition in Sonnet 15:

> *Everything that grows*
> *Holds in perfection but a little moment.*

The Buddhist belief in impermanence reflects this universal realization. So does mindfulness, since it is usually experienced in moment-by-moment awarenesses, in which we are finally free from what appear to be stable conditions. Only in such unconditioned moments can unconditional love become a believable possibility for us.

A term from algebra may help us be more exact about mindful moments of you-and-I relating. An asymptote is a curve that gets increasingly closer to a line on a graph *without ever reaching it.* The word in Greek means "never intersecting." Perhaps this is a more accurate description of what happens in intimate moments. We keep getting closer, but never fully achieve the I-thou experience. At best, we achieve approximations. This algebraic term gives hope to those of us who have noticed how well-nigh impossible an absolutely authentic recognition of another and a total presence can really be. There is no total merger, no unmediated perception, no complete escape from conditioned consciousness—but we can keep getting better. We can bracket our mind-sets, transferences, and projections long enough to see well enough, and we can let that be enough.

Mindfulness is a moment-by-moment awareness, so brevity is legitimate. Mindfulness is appropriate etiquette in the midst of life's impermanence. Mindfulness helps us love in a transitory world. One of the most touching things about us humans is that even though we realize the truth of impermanence and near-missing of each other, that cannot stop us from loving with all our might, from bonding with each other with what Shakespeare calls "hoops of steel." This is not illogical, mistaken, foolish, or tragic. It is how we override the condition of impermanence with unconditional love. It is how love lives on, whether or not lovers do.

In any case, no moment is ever trivial, since any moment points to the exit into enlightenment. Indeed, awakening is a moment in which we glimpse the unconditioned mind, what Buddha called "nirvana," a complete freedom from attachment, the result of our utter letting go of irrational fear and addictive desire. William Wordsworth saw this as:

> *A flash of the invisible world:*
> *'Twas a moment's pause,*
> *All that took place within me came and went*
> *As in a moment . . . .*

Practice
Presence, Mindfulness, and Loving-kindness

Here are the psychological practices that help us begin to work through our transferences. They are the same steps that can help in working on relationship problems when we practice them with a partner. They are the prerequisites for presence, mindfulness, and loving-kindness.

- We begin by simply noticing the physical facts about others as they are in this very moment: he is standing; he is talking; he is waving his arms; he is looking to the right. This practice of ruthless focus on the bare here-and-now reality is a way to break through transference because we limit our focus to what is, rather than let ourselves be seduced by what we are projecting. Projection seems to make everything definite and unalterable; attention to the here and now shows us how everything keeps changing.

- Allied to this is asking someone what she is really saying or feeling, or repeating what we hear to make sure we understood her. We ask her if we got it right. This corrects any possible fantasy or transference into a reality.
- Whenever possible we make our transference conscious and call ourselves on it, acknowledging the object of our transference as a spin-off of earlier stories. We ask ourselves, "Who is she like?"
- We ask others to point out what they may see as our transferences onto them.
- We notice when we are trying to find in others what we lost out on in childhood. We pay attention to how we are trying to recapture moments so we can redo them or be done with them. Simply pointing and naming in that conscious way makes an exponential impact on clearing up our comedy of errors.

We commit ourselves to addressing, processing, resolving, and integrating our transferences, as was outlined in the practices section at the end of chapter 2.

Learning to be *present* to someone without the interferences of transference consists first in setting an ongoing intention to be present fully in an I-to-you way. When we are then actually with others, we can check in with ourselves by ticking down the list of the five A's:

Am I paying *attention* or am I planning what will I say next? Am I on the defensive rather than open? Am I noticing feelings and body language, or am I hearing only words?

Am I *accepting* him as he is, or passing a judgment on his lifestyle or behavior?

Do I *appreciate* her, or am I devaluing or minimizing her? Do I see her worth and cherish it? Do I value the place she has in my life, or am I taking her for granted?

Do I feel *affection—that is, friendliness*—or do I fear closeness and therefore distance myself from her? Do I show physical affection in appropriate ways? Do I show intimacy by holding and touching, or do I show it only through sex?

Am I *allowing* him to be himself, or am I trying to control his behavior by censuring him for his choices or orientation in life?

We may notice two common automatic styles of behavior that interfere with allowing: We see something or someone appealing and want to grab and cling. This is attachment, the result of neediness. Alternatively, we are scared or repelled and want to run: "Get me out of here."

In authentic presence we let go of the grab-and-cling style in favor of allowing something or someone to come and go at will. We let go of addictive clinging while still being able to hold and relate to others. For instance, we stay in relationship with a relaxed rather than controlling grasp so that the other feels free and yet connected.

We let go of the "get me out of here" escape by allowing ourselves simply to stay with what is happening, to let it have its full career of feelings in us. When we repress our feelings or hide from reality, we are aggressively attempting to control ourselves and the world. For example, we fear finding out about our health status, so we avoid appropriate testing. Instead, we can bite the bullet and be tested, feeling all the feelings that go with the experience.

- *Mindfulness* is practiced first in daily meditation, in which we sit silently and simply notice our thoughts rather than entertaining or rejecting them. Our tendency is to entertain the appealing thoughts and dispel the unappealing thoughts. When we treat them as equal, we begin to lose track of our tendency to grab on to or escape events and emotions that arise in the course of the day. We can tolerate what is unpleasant; we do not have to become addicted to what is pleasurable. This is how the mindful style of dealing with thoughts helps us find equanimity in life, an imperturbability in the face of storm and stress. We are no longer swayed by what beckons or repels; we are no longer conditioned selves but rather unconditionally present to what is, in its purest spaciousness.

  We are also letting go of the mind-sets that are so common in our daily thoughts: fear of what might befall us, desire to hold on, judgment of others, attempts to control others or control the predicaments life presents to us, and finally indulgence in illusion rather than loyalty to life as it is and to others as they are.

We bring what we experience in meditation into our daily lives, both cognitively and behaviorally. Mindfulness affects us cognitively in that it is paying attention without labeling. Mind-sets are "thoughts about." Mindfulness is awareness of how we think. We begin to see just how thought and reality are constructed, and we smile benignly. Mind-sets evoke stressful feeling reactions based on fear or desire. Mindfulness changes our emotional experience so we can be present without reacting from such compulsions. Mind-sets seek out what is pleasant and avoid what is unpleasant, thereby attempting to control experience. Mindfulness shows us ways of tolerating any experience so that our fears can be dispelled and our desires can be less demanding. The customary escapes are relinquished in favor of openness to what is. This inviting of the ever-flowing newness into our lives releases us from the need for projection and transference.

We can't expunge the past from the present. Yet in mindfulness, we can relate to the present without being attached to or blinded by the transferences that surround our past experience. We can mindfully detach and disidentify from the transferred past or the feared or desired future. We do this as we label our thoughts and calm our adrenaline reactiveness rather than oppose or entertain them.

- *Loving-kindness/metta* is a practice in Buddhism by which we may wish four immeasurable spiritual gifts to ourselves and others: love, compassion, joy, and equanimity. We intend each of these, one at a time, first for ourselves, then for those we love, then for those to whom we may be indifferent, then for those with whom we have difficulties, and finally for all beings. Our arc of love thus widens from our own hearts to those of all humanity. What seemed so separate now appears as it really is, one. Our common human goal of happiness makes us realize our oneness.

  We can use this same practice by beaming kind thoughts and wishes to those who hurt or disturb us. Loving-kindness is not an alternative to standing up for ourselves; it is an addition. We stand up for ourselves and we complete our transaction with others by aspirations that they may find the qualities that lead to enlightenment.

We can design the loving-kindness practice in a variety of ways. Loving-kindness is an attitude of friendliness and warmth toward all beings. It also shows itself in our behavior. We act in ways that promote the good of others rather than only our own self-interest. When our loving-kindness notices someone's happiness, it attunes to it rather than envying it. When our loving-kindness encounters pain, it transforms into compassion. When our loving-kindness is struck by how upset and out of control people become, it transmutes itself into equanimity and wishes that for them. Thus loving-kindness helps us experience and extend to others at the same time.

We combine mindfulness and loving-kindness as we look into the pure reality of who we are rather than be caught in our concepts, biases, and beliefs. We rest in openness to openness. Perfect love happens in that nameless domain. When we try to love outside it, in the restricted land of projections, transferences, and expectations, we fail, since we are exiled from the only land where love can be born. It is the land with no national name, established religion, ethnic purity, geographical boundary. There, with our passport of loving-kindness, we welcome everyone under one sky, on one earth.

As our practice of loving-kindness takes hold in us, it becomes a commitment, even a calling. Then, in all that happens to us and in every way others treat us, we see opportunities to love more. Every issue and person becomes an opening of our hearts.

Create a small piece of paradise here on earth by loving and embracing each other and by loving and embracing the whole world. The cruelty, chaos, and pain of daily living cannot dim your vision of everlasting, perfect love as long as you maintain your precious friendships.
        —Saint Aelred

4

Reactions and Reacting

Persons, Pets, Places, and Things

What does a cell phone mean to a child whose parents interrupt their time with him to take incoming calls?

What does a refrigerator mean to a child when it is usually empty or stocked only with beer?

What does the television mean to an adult who was once a latchkey child?

Transference is not limited to persons. It can happen between us and any animal, event/ritual, place, or thing. We attach feeling-laden meanings to things.

A toddler finds independence as he walks away from mother, but he carries a blanket that retains her warmth and perhaps her smell. This is how he feels secure. The blanket or teddy bear is called a "transitional object." A thing becomes a metaphor for caring and safety.

All through life we use transitional objects to comfort us and to maintain connections that we believe are necessary to our existence. We refer to and treat our possessions as if they were extensions of ourselves. We use our possessions, and sometimes our relationships or our children, to establish a sense of stability. We picture God as a human person who watches us or watches out for us. These are all metaphors, all forms of transference.

A pet, a car, a child may re-create and represent an original crucial connection we never want to lose fully. Indeed, we came into existence because of a connection, that of our parents' intercourse. Inasmuch as transference shows us how deeply and pervasively everything in our life is connected, it perhaps can be called a psychological ecology.

We all see that some *things* in adult life are now like teddy bears and we clutch them for a sense of safety—for example, a ring, a rosary, a photo, a memento. This is not a sign of weakness but a recognition that things indeed hold meanings, and wonderfully so, meanings that can be counted on for some relief in painful times. Problems arise only when things are seen as magical or as substitutes for our own commitment to taking action in a way that would enable us to face our predicaments in adult ways.

Perhaps you lived in Boston in your student days and now recall it with nostalgia. You associate Boston with free-spirited living, and imagine that if you go back there, you will find that same old sense of joyous liberation waiting for you. Actually, you are transferring onto a city the affect that goes with youth. A place has remained dear because of transference, not necessarily because it will still be so wonderful to us. "That same old . . . " is not the same when we are old.

Food is part of the transfer of affect. Perhaps we reconnect with our warm feelings from childhood in what we call "comfort food." We can tell the difference between the bubble gum we bought on our own in childhood and the special food served at home by nurturing parents or grandparents. Both came from the same era, but only the latter has strong affect attached to it now. We associate comfort with eating foods that came to us in the context of secure and reliable bonding.

Holidays carry a potential for transference. We recall our childhood Christmases as joyous or perhaps as disappointing. Now when Christmas comes around, we feel either overly excited or depressed, or both. Our original experience still designs our reactions to the here and now. In the example of Christmas, we meet up with the issues of giving and receiving, as well as comings and goings—troubled areas for most people. We recall not getting enough or getting too much. We carry a bodily resonance of that experience in our unconscious, and it arises in the form of emotional reactions every December until we work it out and let it go. Then Christmas becomes a new holiday with implications and meanings that we now find or ascribe to it, disentangled from past connotations. This is experiencing Christmas as it is for us in the present, not as it was for us in the past.

Pets are certainly apt objects of transference. A dog will comfort us, provide a sense of connection, love us unconditionally, keep us company, cheer us up, remain loyal, and certainly be more of an expert at giving the five A's than many humans. We begin to see our pets as persons, sometimes as our children or as partners. We become attached and are deeply concerned about their safety and health. They become important to our happiness. Human needs are being fulfilled by an animal. There is nothing wrong in any of this, but it is useful to notice the transference dimension. How much of our sense of isolation is being made up for by Spot's faithful presence when Dick or Jane have left us? We can trust to "see Spot run" *with* us instead of *away from* us as humans sometimes do. Perhaps this loyalty from Spot can make us feel securely accompanied in life. Transference can then be a reminder of how much we missed in our past. It is also a reminder of how much we have to be thankful for in pets who so reliably and willingly make up for our woeful losses.

We can become very strongly bonded to a pet. Our mind and words say, "Oh, I know we are separate and that she is only a pet." On the visceral level, though, the dog has become a significant other, a family member. Then we take insults to or rejection of our pet personally. This is not in the realm of right or wrong on our part. When we choose to cede territory from our psyche onto a dog, it is then up to us as adults to accept the given that we will now feel bad not only by how others treat us but by how they treat our dog.

Our attitude and way of treating our pets—or our children—may reveal something about how we were treated in our childhood. For instance, our dog barks fiercely when another dog passes by the house. We have been trying to train him not to be so angry. We send him into the bathroom when he barks aggressively, the equivalent perhaps of our parents sending us to our room when we showed anger in childhood?

Another example is even more subtle. We may feel a need to people the house, especially if we live alone, with the same number of beings as in our original home. We thus have two dogs and one cat at home now when in childhood there were four members in our family. A clue to this may be the need very soon to replace a pet who dies. This seems like an avoidance of grief, but it may be an unconscious need to restore the "proper" household population. In this way, the family structure is intact and we are less lonely.

Finally, we remind ourselves that animals in ancient myth were crucial to the heroic journey. Dogs were considered escorts to the underworld, which was a symbol of the unconscious. In Greece, a dog was the guard of the underworld. In modern stories, it was a dog that instigated Dorothy's journey to Oz and helped her to see the true nature of the wizard. It was the white rabbit that led Alice into the underworld of wonders that await those willing to look down under their conscious life. Only when we go to these hidden places do we, like her, discover our unexpected dimensions.

On the Job Too

Workers may transfer onto their boss attitudes or feelings that hearken back to authority figures from childhood or from other employment situations. A worker may be revisited by a bully from childhood in the form of the bully boss he works for now.

Workers might seek approval in too extreme a way or become noncompliant or aggressive. The unfinished emotions from past experiences with authority figures automatically play themselves out in the workplace.

If they are treating their workers like children, managers may be under the spell of transference, derived from how their parents treated them in childhood. A boss might demand personal loyalty in addition to simply getting the job done. It may also be predominantly a case of transference if management fails to attune to the human needs of workers in the workplace.

A matter-of-fact style from a manager to an employee will often lead to resentment because it seems cold and demeaning. This may be a clue to a transference in which a worker expected a manager to treat him as kindly or even as lovingly as one of his parents did. In fact, in any setting, when people communicate in too business-like a way, others will tend to feel as if they are objects of use rather than subjects of respect, as in a you-and-I relationship. As humans, we want to feel loved in all our interactions, even though the givens of life do not promise that. However, to want respect is as reasonable in the workplace as it is in any relationship.

We know that our place of work is a business that survives by making money, but, given our transferences, we automatically feel all these family connections forming there. Meanwhile management may still insist that business is only business. This may easily lead to conflicts between worker and manager, who operate from opposite perspectives and diverse wishes. The irony is that, as Japanese corporations have demonstrated, what is best for business has proven to be a workforce that feels a family bond with management. As we grow in our commitment to human values, we will form businesses not only for profit and job satisfaction but for the well-being and growth of all who work in them.

It is important for a manager/boss to see how he or she may be creating an atmosphere of competition among the workers. It is certainly helpful for workers and managers to be aware of sibling rivalry and transference reactions. As long as transference remains unconscious, it can create stress. Once it is out in the open, we can get to work on changing things for the better.

The more a manager is a healthy, powerful leader, the more we might idealize him and then expect him to be a parent figure with all the nurturing and loyal care that parents provide. In a patriarchal style of interacting, an implicit bargain is made between obedience and caretaking. In the dominator model of management we are expected to go along with company policies in exchange for job safety. When a manager fails to see us as real people and becomes controlling or domineering, we might rebel against him as we would against a parent, shifting from idealizing to demonizing. The transference element of relationships helps us understand how it all works, or fails to work.

The critical words of a partner or boss become less impactful when we are no longer caught in transferences. Attempts at criticism fall flat once the other no longer has familial power over us. We take it all as testimony about him, not as a verdict on us. Less reactiveness means transference is no longer driving or stopping us. (After the following practice, we will look more carefully at the subject of criticism.)

Practice
In the Workplace

A simple technique to discover the presence of transference in your workplace is to think of two positive qualities of your coworker or boss and two negative qualities. Ask yourself how these match with those of your original family members or your former bosses/coworkers or former partner. For example, your manager may be highly critical and seem to be incapable of being pleased by your work. You may recall that your mom was highly critical and your dad could not be pleased. The boss is reviving both experiences at once.

How do we respond as adults? We *pause* when we feel ourselves upset by criticism. We *look for the grain of truth* in the feedback. We *link* the comment to some theme from our past and feel the energy bound up there. Our limbic/emotional reaction then may calm itself into an enlightened moment. We are excited that we have found yet another clue to our inner world as revealed in our reactions to others. We *welcome* the opportunity to stop living anachronistically and to enter the present more deliberately. Sometimes there is no actual issue between us and others, only our own pet issue barking back at us. Then our work is to address, process, resolve, and integrate.

We can laugh at ourselves for how we are still so in awe of the authority figures. Yet we have it in us to be fearless, as in this example: You are sitting at a table in a coffee shop and in walks your third-grade teacher, whom you have not seen in over twenty years. She comes over to your table and instead of greeting you with a smile, she says sternly, "Sit up straight and fold your hands on the table." You do not feel obliged to do it; you take it as a joke and laugh, no matter how she intended it. If we can say no to authoritative control in an instance like that, we can do so, at least in little ways, in other circumstances. We can *practice those little ways* even when the power seems to be entirely in the hands of others.

Finally, we can *remain aware* that work is not always a safe place to practice assertiveness. The rules in some jobs do not permit speaking up easily or at all, nor do they allow or foster a healthy openness. If a workplace is intimidating and antihumanistic, it is up to us to *find a better situation* for ourselves, if at all possible. If that is not possible, we suffer from the ongoing stress and can certainly bolster ourselves with stress-reduction techniques, though these cannot serve as a complete remedy.

To be exhausted every day after work, to be full of anxiety about the politics at work, to be disrespected by management or fellow workers—situations like these make our workplace a hell. It is then an inappropriate setting for human beings who want to grow in self-esteem and maintain their physical health. It is up to us to do what we can to make our workplace more humanistic or to find work elsewhere. Our bodies pay dearly later for all the stress and frustration, just as they may still be paying for a dysfunctional childhood or relationship.

The rules of fair play, the healthy psychological techniques we have learned from the self-help movement, the advances in spiritual consciousness we have made in our adult lives—these important principles and more may be totally nonexistent or even not permitted in a workplace. All bets are off in some jobs and with some managers. It is up to us to decide whether our paycheck is worth the pain that some jobs inflict on us.

The Critic Within

What am I still believing about myself that is a carryover from the past rather than something that serves me now?

In this book, we have looked at tools and steps that help us work through transferences. Now we look into ourselves to see the carryovers, the parental messages from our past that remain inside us today and likewise need clearing. How do we understand and then confront our own inner critic? How do we talk back rather than sit still for the lies and half-truths?

Criticism is the opposite of acknowledgment, which is what we all want. Criticism hurts us because it cancels all three parts of the trio of mirroring. We are not nurtured, not held in our inadequacy, but instead shamed for it. We are not understood for all that we are, but instead only for the one area that is being judged. And we certainly feel disconnected from the other.

When parents or former partners were continually judgmental of or humiliating toward us, we might have introjected their disparagements. *Introject* comes from a Latin word that means "to toss inside." Thus we take what hits us from others' criticisms and put it so far into ourselves that we believe it is now originating in us. This is endorsed as we hear it in our own voice, coming from within our own minds. We clobber ourselves with others' weapons.

Critical remarks that become introjected are those that shame us with our failures rather than help us overcome them. Such remarks are characterized by a global and timeless attribution: we are "all bad" and always have been. The sense of helplessness we felt when these statements hailed down on us can lead us later to overcompensate by trying to be in control of everything in life.

We do not develop our own critical sense until age seven, so what we heard from parents entered our psyche and stayed there, no matter how insulting or degrading. We lacked the tools to pick and choose what we would let in. After age seven, we might still have believed what was said to us because of our sense of duty to parental authority and our fear of losing their approval. This accounts for our inner self-criticisms becoming so ingrained, enduring, and far-reaching. The true self is delicate, easily browbeaten by years of brainwashing into believing how dangerous its emergence would be. It willingly goes underground until it hears the "all clear" that comes from the five A's of love from someone we trust or from ourselves.

Our mother is both an historical character and an interior character. To clear a mother's criticisms now takes clearing the internalized version of her, the imago of her critical self within us. Transference gives us opportunities to do this through others, but it is a dangerous game. It is more responsible and efficient to pursue it as our own work on ourselves and not through facsimiles.

The danger is not in the memory of mother's words as she said them but in how we hold on to the critical voice today or look for those who will imitate it. We do so because criticism is familiar, a connection with the past that grants a sense of continuity. We still maintain a loyalty to the only parents we had, no matter how inadequate. We are fighting all that when we flee the voice that has become so much a part of us.

A strong inner critic makes the criticisms we hear from others in our present life come at us with heavier weight. However, as we work on ourselves, that begins to change. For instance, our mother's present-day criticisms no longer impinge upon us as they did in the past. If they still bruise and provoke, we are not quite done with our work. Here is what "the work is done" looks like: Her words become flatlined, a recall of memory, information about who she still is, no longer a disempowering blow upon us. What was before so power-packed now has lost its charge. The wounding words no longer find a way in. The new center of evaluation of our behavior becomes what we hear from our own conscience, not from what others think of us, no matter how closely related to us. We have regained our power, our sense of personal authority.

Family members may criticize us when we share about ourselves candidly or when we want to discuss serious topics. A healthy response is to recognize that such conversation is impossible and becomes toxic, frustrating, or hurtful to us. It then becomes necessary to limit our conversations to small talk. We take care of ourselves best when we know the limitations of others and act accordingly. We stay away from any subject that may lead to criticism of us or to inappropriate feelings in others. This is not cowardice on our part. It is a respect for the right time and place for free speech and a wise way to keep the peace.

We may notice that a certain relative constantly says mean things to us or criticizes us. The relationship between us seems toxic, and we wonder if there is some magic word that we can say that will stop her and open a real dialogue. Perhaps we have spoken up but nothing has worked. The practice then turns to ourselves: We stay anchored in our own integrity by not retaliating and not spending more time with her than is necessary. In addition, we include her by name in our loving-kindness practice.

A critical view of us is often based on a family bias about us, on how we appeared in childhood. Here is an example of how three siblings might labor under a family myth about themselves: One is considered miserly, even though she gives her fair share and even more than the others as the years go by. Another is considered intellectually not very bright, even though she has upgraded her intelligence with recent education and life experience. A third is considered a liar, even though she now tells the truth. Most families maintain their own original impression of who we are, and it becomes a bias from which we cannot be fully exonerated. This is an example of how the need to repeat becomes like spinning our wheels. The alternative would have been to begin with the five A's rather than with looking for things to shame us for. Shaming is the opposite of loving.

Strangely, in transference, we look for partners and relationship scenarios that might confirm the family myth about us. Repealing the family myth may feel to us like disloyalty to our parents or family. The village-rooted part of our psyche fears that option, since with it comes the image of ourselves as pariahs, orphans, exiles. How ironic that we are fearing the very archetypes that in mythology represent stepping out and self-renewal.

The *inner* critic is the main culprit. He has believed the myth and now seeks to prove it. This internalized criticism—self-shaming—induces us to fear our own inner motives and impulses and to turn against them. We become judges and executioners rather than caring ombudsmen for or fair witnesses of our behavior. Inner beliefs become so habitual that we come to believe they are valid. Inner judgments become so habitual that we come to believe they are deserved.

Our emphasis on the inner critic cannot preclude an honest look at ourselves: We can still grow so much in self-knowledge by being ruthlessly honest about ourselves. We can indeed be arrogant, mean, prone to repetition of mistakes, selfish in our demands on others. We have been this way before and can be again. We seek neither punishment nor full pardon but openness to our ongoing human condition of confusion and occasional misdeeds. We grow spiritually when we balance our willingness to admit our shortcomings with a commitment to keep working with ourselves. Indeed, commitment means continual dedication to the work, not once-and-for-all accomplishment. That dedication is such a clearly lighted and direct path to serenity, sanity, and awakening.

Finally, people with a strong inner critic are often also hypercritical of others. It is a spiritual practice to check in with ourselves, to examine our words and behavior and notice if we are being condemnatory. The danger in judging others is threefold:

- We hurt people's feelings.
- When we see others as stereotypes or jump to conclusions about them, we may not grasp what they have come to teach us. We also miss out on intimate moments with them and on noticing how unique, how touching their story is. These are the qualities that can open us to compassion.

- When we criticize, we stand to lose compassion for the difficult conditions that are behind what others may do.

The less we criticize, the more loving-kindness can arise in our hearts. Could it be that we judge others so that we will not feel the full impact of that power of love? Could it be that others criticize us because they don't want to love us quite so much?

Practice
Releasing Ourselves from Our Myths

We cannot easily replace a negative voice with a positive one. Our healing happens when we notice our critical inner voice, peg it as only a thought with no authority, and then make room for constructive feedback to ourselves. We then hear a favorite uncle inside rather than a critical parent. We take responsibility for our behavior and make amends if we have acted unjustly. But we can also see when we are innocent, and rejoice in our integrity. Then the critic becomes the advocate, the indwelling spirit rather than the demeaning tyrant. This does not happen when we cancel one belief in favor of its opposite. Rather we *allow believability* of an opposite to penetrate us. For instance, if an inner critical voice tells us we are not lovable, we affirm our lovability. This is the equivalent of trusting that Buddha mind or being, consciousness, bliss, or an indwelling Spirit is our authentic and ineradicable true nature.

A painful or abusive childhood may have forced us to hold the opposites of wanting to run away and having to stay. In adult life, we may then associate holding opposites with powerlessness. This mindset can disable us from embracing the tension of opposites, which is so crucial to our psychological and spiritual progress.

Myths of self-criticism thrive on beliefs about ourselves usually inherited from those who shamed or blamed us. We can now instead be moved not by what we believe but by what the record shows. A string of successes, an enduring style of making the best of things, a series of choices based on the best advice available, a commitment to finding a loving response to whatever happens to us—these are all entries on our record.

They mean so much more than the verdicts that our mind construes. A perfect example is one I heard regarding Judy Garland. She was a great and versatile entertainer by worldwide opinion, yet she doubted her talent and feared that she would be found out. The list of successful films, songs, and stage shows are the record. Fears that do not match the record are groundless. Consider this distinction and write up your own record in your journal.

Sometimes the critical words of someone give us helpful feedback about a trait of ours that truly does need to be addressed and changed. We can look directly at the message, not getting caught up in the negative censure. In such mindfulness we go directly to the useful information. (In fact, what is useful is often more valuable than what is true.) We take it to heart and show thanks for it. We trust that we can alter our behavior to act more wholesomely. We also believe that we contain the positive quality that is the opposite of the negative one that has been pointed out to us. Indeed, virtues grow from their opposites: courage from fear faced, love from hate faced down, wisdom from confusion welcomed. Our worst traits—and mistakes—are doors to King Solomon's mines.

This is in keeping with the Buddhist realization about the co-arising of all conditions and qualities: Our ego trait of aggression is balanced within us by access to wise nonviolence. The vulture of fear is never alone on the branch. Beside him is always the eagle of fearlessness. Our inclination to evil inhabits our souls equally with our inherent goodness. Our focus moves from the barb of the truth-based criticism to the truth of an alternative possibility. That evokes the joy that repels sticks and stones.

The critical voice is in words, which hearken from the left hemisphere of our brain. We can also activate our right hemisphere by focusing on a sense of our body as a whole and its physical steadiness, a symbol of our stability as persons of integrity. This leads to a calm abiding in reality. We then affirm, "Joy and safety are arising in me when before there was fear and danger." That will be felt as a physical shift, and we will know we have finally come home to our bodies.

Our body joins in the process when we pay immediate attention to our posture. We stand or sit up straight as soon as the inner critic—or anyone—begins to criticize us. This contributes greatly to our sense of ourselves as fully adult rather than as the child being scolded.

Comforting ourselves with the statement that the inner critic is "only in the mind" makes our mind seem paltry and is another put-down. Our mind is the locus of enlightenment. When our mind is cleared of alien voices and focused on contributing to the development of a healthy ego, it becomes a wonderful tool. We can acknowledge that and change our statement to "This inner critic is a stowaway in my mind, and I am ready to deport him."

We can recall the importance of our spiritual practices. Spiritual practices equip us to experience happiness without attachment. They also serve to let us recall being hurt without the desire for revenge. Thus, regarding recollection of being judged or shamed, we can form an intention of loving-kindness and compassion toward those who maligned us. This is another way of letting go of attachment, both to blame of others and to the internalizing of their verdicts.

We may have been treated in childhood or in a relationship as if we were strange, different, or unacceptable. We may have been told that something was wrong with us. We can reframe that now as we work on clearing those atavistic critical messages: "I always had a unique path. I was always different because there is a special creativity in me that was clamoring to be activated in a hard-of-hearing world. The fact that I still feel like an outsider may be how this creative urge has remained alive in me. I am thankful for it and want to open myself to it now. And since I know how it feels to be excluded, may I not exclude others. Let my painful path be one that leads me to care about others." The final two sentences are how the loving-kindness practice figures in.

Myths from which we cannot be redeemed can make childhood family gatherings unappealing. Do we stay away altogether? Our adult challenge is to maintain the connection but not become caught in a dependency. Our adult challenge is to be respectful but not obligated. How do we accomplish this? How do we let go of codependency with respect to our families of origin?

- We stay in communication, especially on holidays and birthdays, by phone, and briefly if necessary. We only show up in person if we can be sure that the experience will be favorable to our mental health.

- We are always respectful.
- We do not use comebacks, nor do we retaliate in any way.
- We do not use relatives for financial gain, thereby becoming dependent upon them.
- We act in a caring and responsible way when family members are sick or dying. This means seeing to their care but not necessarily providing it personally.
- We no longer lead from our injuries but from the inviolable and inextricable capacity within us to love and be loved.

Why Others Get to Us as They Do

Transference is not all there is to our relationships at home or at work. It is simply one of the four most common dimensions that appear in our reactions to others: We meet up with our (1) shadow side, (2) our ego, or (3) our early or any past experience (the realm of transference). However, we might also act from (4) our authentic self, the self that shows and receives the five A's; we engage in you-and-I relating.

We can look at each of these four in turn:

1. Negatively, the *shadow* refers to the unacceptable impulses we have repressed in ourselves but see so disturbingly in others. Positively, the shadow consists of the gifts/talents/virtues that we disavow in ourselves and admire so much in others. We imagine that what is in ourselves is actually out there in others. Thus our shadow combines what we reject and project. Actually, we have thrown ("projected") parts of who we are onto others. Assumptions about people are also forms of projection.

Just as we can become conscious of transference, we can become conscious of our shadow and learn about our hidden or disavowed self from what we dislike or admire in others. We do this by withdrawing our projections and bringing them back to ourselves. Once we acknowledge our dark, negative traits or positive gifts, we make friends with our hitherto unnoticed self. We see both the Hitler and the Mother Teresa in ourselves and then we take responsibility for our own inclinations and choices, both dark and light. We no longer deplore or adore others so vigorously. We locate the full spectrum of human possibility in ourselves.

As we take back our projections, an enormous creativity opens in us. We continue to admire others but not at the expense of self-appreciation. We still see others' negative traits but realize we have some too. Then we appreciate the shadow as a positive path to finding kernels of personal creativity in the dark corners of others and self-actualization in our overly spotlighted idols. We are all everything; projection prevents us from seeing or believing in the full spectrum of our own light.

2. We may find that our entitled arrogant *ego* has been activated by someone's behavior toward us. This is the autocrat within who demands full control over other people, events, and predicaments. This inflated ego beguiles us into believing that we are above the givens of life and are entitled to an exemption from them. The inflated ego is the part of us that becomes insulted and vengeful when we are criticized or when we are crossed in our attempts to force things to come out our way. This narcissistic ego is apt to make us hold on to any slight and to keep looking for ways to vindicate and avenge ourselves. This is the part of us that wants to make a divorce hostile "to show her she can't treat *me* that way and get away with it." We work on our shadow by befriending it. We work on taming our egos by spiritual practices. (One of my previous books may be helpful in these areas: *Shadow Dance: Liberating the Power and Creativity of Your Dark Side*.)

3. We may also react to others by transference, in which our *early life issues* or *earlier relationship issues* come back to find us through what sounds like our father's severe or gentle voice, our mother's or former partner's warm or too-fleeting embrace. We work on transference by making the similarity between past and present conscious, admitting the truth of what we have been caught up in, and ceasing to act in ways that make the transference interactions persist.

- It may be our *shadow* that is reacting to others' unacceptable behavior when we guess or wonder, "I may be like that too."
- We can suppose it is our *ego* that is reacting to others' unacceptable behavior when we say or think, "How *dare* she do this to *me*?"
- Our *early life* may be coming back as transference when we feel, "Dad/Mom did this same thing to me." Ironically, we often wind up doing the very same thing to others that our parents or former partners did to us.

4. Finally, sometimes we live purely in the moment with no shadow or ego projections in the way. There is no transference, only this person as himself or this behavior as itself. Then we experience *you-and-I* relating. This may take one of two forms:

First, an interaction or an ongoing relationship with someone can be virtually free of shadow projections, ego competition, or transference issues. We simply relate in matter-of-fact or friendly ways without the usual neurotic obstructions and deceptions.

Secondly, you-and-I relating can happen as true intimacy. We see someone in her authentic reality and show her ours. This is usually interspersed with interruptions by the shadow or by ego or by transference. But it can last just long enough for us to feel the exuberant freedom of being in the here and now with someone really herself rather than with a displaced person.

We have all seen the pictures of Jesus with his heart on the outside, his entire inner self open and offered to the viewer. This is a metaphor for spiritual, in-depth relating. In an I-to-you moment a heart connection opens and we approach the core self of the other. The word *heart* in Latin is *cor*: The core of someone is the heart we may have waited a lifetime to find. We offer the same in return. The result is an accuracy in relating rather than a reflection of a dark side of ourselves, an ideal or enemy of our egos, or an understudy for dad or big sister.

Not only is the enlightened state in us, so is the unconditional love we so much want to find. In the you-and-I moment, a mutual unconditional love can be released. *It is unconditional because it is not conditioned by shadow or ego projection or by transference.*

Practice
Seeing What Gets in the Way

As a practice, we can ask ourselves to S.E.E. what is going on between ourselves and others: "What is being activated here, my Shadow, my Ego, or my Earlier experiences now revived in transference?" In fact, this same technique can be helpful whenever we become upset and don't quite know what is going on in us. This practice helps make us responsible for our feelings. From such a nonblaming stance, we are more likely to contact and express our loving-kindness. It will flow out all by itself without great effort.

Practice
Opening

Here is a simple threefold skill for dealing with what upsets us. Notice that openness is the skillful means we will employ rather than ego-engineering what we feel, which is actually a form of aggressive control. To be open to a full experience breaks the ego's habit of self-centralizing.

We begin by noticing what we feel. We also notice how much force is in our reaction or in how we feel or show it. This means listening to ourselves and holding our experience rather than overriding it with defenses or excuses, running from it, blaming others or retaliating against them for how we are feeling. This is how we admit, always the first step.

Second, we ask, "What is the message here? What work do I need to do on myself? What shadow, ego, or transference issue does this experience point to?"

Finally, we say, "Yes. Now what?"

All three of these steps are forms of *opening.*

In the first step, by noticing, I am open to seeing what I feel. I am opening to my own truth.

In the second step, I am opening to what I can learn and how I am responsible.

In the third step, I am opening to the challenges of accepting my own reality and then getting on with my life in a productive way.

Practice
F.A.C.E.-ing Ourselves

We can also practice awareness of how and when our ego becomes aroused and we can let go of its stressful domination over our thoughts or actions. The neurotic *ego* is the face we are trying to save: F.A.C.E.—fear, attachment, control, and entitlement. When we are upset, we can practice ticking down our F.A.C.E. list to see if and how our ego has been provoked. We look at what has upset us and ask ourselves:

What am I afraid of?
What am I attached to getting or proving?
What am I trying to control?
What do I think I am entitled to?

We meet the challenge to let go of ego with a practice of loving-kindness. We then ask:

How can my fear and defensiveness become love and openness?
How can my attachment turn into letting go?
How can I allow others to be who they are and let things unfold as they will, rather than try to control people and events?
How can I let go of my attitude of entitlement and instead responsibly stand up for my rights and let go without seeking reprisals if they cannot be secured?

This is accepting the given that life can be unfair no matter how assertive we are. Our psychological commitment is to no capitulation; our spiritual commitment is to no retaliation. *This practice is a spiritual alchemy, since the leaden ego becomes the gold of the loving Self.*

Practice
Searching Questions

Dealing with reactions takes self-knowledge. The following hard-hitting questions help us know the unique characteristics of our present life. We can ask whether they are givens to work with or habits to reconsider. Answering these questions honestly helps us inventory ourselves so we can know ourselves better. This gives us a basis for accepting present facts about ourselves, the best position from which to make changes in ourselves so we can live more happily. Answer these questions in your journal and then share them with someone you trust. (The first question simply calls for a deeper acceptance of ourselves, because it seems to be part of our psychological DNA.)

• Am I mostly an introvert or mostly an extrovert or evenly both?
  Do I notice with some people or in some situations that I am
  more introverted than extroverted or vice versa?

- Is my definition of self-esteem based on how much others admire me or on how accurately I portray myself, inadequacies and all?
- In the course of life, have I found myself mostly in leadership positions, or do I do better as a support person in projects?
- Have I mostly sought partners who would be parents to me, children to me, or peers of mine?
- Do I tend to see the humor and playfulness in events, or do I tend to see a darker side?
- Have things come easily to me and worked out for me in my life, or has it been pretty much an uphill climb?
- Do I express feelings easily and openly, or do I tend to hold them in?
- Do I see myself as having an addictive personality? Do I routinely deny myself? Am I able to act in moderation?
- Do I mostly find myself carefully planning, or do I act impulsively?
- With respect to money, am I usually spendthrift, generous, stingy, overly indebted, or appropriate?
- In intimate relationships, do I give with healthy boundaries, or am I codependent? Do I receive with gratitude, or with a sense of entitlement? Am I mostly a giver, or mostly a receiver?
- What is my sexual style? Is there a match between my sexual style in daily life, in my orientation, in my fantasy life?
- Have I mostly found work that fulfills me, or that simply makes me a living?
- What is the spiritual path I am on and what are my spiritual practices?

Practice
From Trigger to Anchor

Here is an additional practice that can be useful when we notice that our buttons are being pushed. Our reactions are triggered by what others say or do or by how they treat us. For instance, when someone comes at us with an aggressive voice or gestures, we may be triggered into fear, hearkening back to our parents' manner toward us in childhood. However, we can meet these triggers of transference with *anchors*—words or actions that help us remain stable. The best anchors are the words of the loving-kindness practice: "May I be free of fear and may this person be free of the need to intimidate." Soon we notice that the words or gestures of the other person are simply passing through us rather than wounding us. This is how love helps us become stronger.

> *I want to unfold. I do not want to remain folded up anywhere, because wherever I am still folded, I am untrue.*
> —Rainer Maria Rilke

Handling Others' Reactions to Us

So far in this book we have been looking at how we as individuals transfer potent, unresolved feelings from the past onto people in our present-day lives. But of course we're not the only ones reliving the past in our relationships. What about when other people react to us out of their old emotional wounds?

Other people transfer onto us in two ways:

First, those onto whom we transfer do so in return. In psychoanalysis, this is called "countertransference" and it happens in most close relationships. Then we are at the mercy of unconscious forces, and you-and-I intimacy becomes difficult. For instance, I may distrust my new partner because she unconsciously reminds me of my former partner, who cheated on me. She herself was distrusted by her father in childhood, so she reacts to me with anger and indignation. We are both caught in the past while believing we are firmly in the present.

Second, some people transfer feelings and expectations onto us while we see them only in a matter-of-fact way. This can happen at work or in other social settings. For instance, I may notice that someone has it in for me or seems obsessed with me and I wonder how I created such an enormous reaction, since this is someone I have hardly noticed until now. A transference reaction to us can be a way of calling us to attention, especially to compassionate attention.

We are not always seeing transference in the reactions of others toward us. Some of those reactions are transference, but some are simply useful feedback. *Mirroring* is the term used for a parent's receptive understanding of a child's needs and feelings, a matching of need with fulfillment. Such mirroring in childhood helped us understand what we really felt. We continue to learn about ourselves from others' reactions and responsiveness to us. Mirroring of our feelings makes us comfortable in this shared world and eases our sense of isolation. This is why feedback is so important to our growth all through life. The ego that cannot handle feedback is thus a disability.

Here are four ways in which negative transference (others' negative reactions to us) shows itself:

1. Others compete or compare themselves to us and exaggerate the differences between themselves and us to make themselves superior. Perhaps someday all of us may let go of the compulsion to win and thereby finally find out how to *play*. Neuroscience has demonstrated that play, which may begin at age three months, is connected to an intense burst of brain development. Humor and playfulness were always pathways to growth, and still are once we are no longer driven so feverishly by the competitive urge.

2. The urgent need on the part of others to rescue or fix us may be a ploy to avoid or manage their own pain. They may be trying to win approval from their own inner parent by proving their competence as caregivers. People seek approval first in person and later in the imago of the person they carry in the locket of their psyche.

3. Some people cannot understand or even see certain features of our personality or behavior. These blind spots may even prevent them from recognizing how much we care about them or from being open to our constructive feedback.

4. Bias and hate can be a manifestation of transference. Some people may show moralistic reactions to our choices or our sexual or political orientation. Some people may have overly strong reactions to our looks, clothing, or mannerisms.

In all four of these examples, something is being stirred up from the personal past of the other onto us. We trigger an emotional reaction in them based on their unresolved emotional wounds.

Practice
Power in Responding

How do we respond to countertransference in healthy and spiritually conscious ways?

In therapy, countertransference does not usually refer to appropriate feelings but to reactions to a client that might induce a therapist to cross a boundary, bestow special privileges, or sabotage treatment. The therapist avoids these pitfalls and restrains herself from reacting to her own overly negative or positive reactions to her client. She speaks of her transference to her supervisor and is silent about it with her client. In personal life, we do not have to be silent. We can speak up, but in a kindly and carefully timed way. To say baldly, "I am not your mother; get over it; see me as me," usually sounds critical and interferes with healthy communication.

It is important to validate the perception of the one who is transferring onto us, to see how it makes sense in some way. *How am I really like his former partner?* Only then do we move from transference into an I-you moment. Here is what the practice may sound like: "I understand how you see your first wife in me. I can see where it comes from. And let us now open to the possibility of a view in which I can be myself and we can meet as you-and-I, not as you-and-she. I don't want to be the latest version of your ex-wife or your mom. I want to be myself so you can see and love me as I am. I want to do the same for you. I know this will take time. Will you make time for me?"

The other person may be quite unaware of the signals she is emitting. Many people are surprised when we reveal their transferences to them. It is up to us to take responsibility for our interpretation of our transference. It is up to us to *explain*. Explanations without defensiveness contribute to authentic intimacy. An explanation is a launching pad for deeper truth between people, especially when it reports feelings and meanings without blame or making anyone wrong.

In negative transference reactions to us, we may notice how others impose their wishes or ego demands on us without an openness to dialogue about what is going on transference-wise. This may take the form of any of the layers of the neurotic ego: intimidation, blame, censure, the need to control or fix us. These are ways by which ego perpetuates our suffering.

Maintaining our boundaries is a reliable way for us to scale these tiers of others' projections. Boundaries help us avoid being manipulated, blindsided, or railroaded by people who are controlling or predatory. Such people often know exactly who will put up with abuse. The wily prince may have wanted Cinderella not because her foot fit the glass slipper but because he knew from the story of her life with her stepmother and stepsisters that she had a capacity to put up with unacceptable behavior.

As we grow in psychological and spiritual consciousness, we *notice* when someone is trying to control or censure us. We do not let that happen, but neither do we blame or retaliate against that person. We simply respond by saying, "Ouch!" and protecting our boundaries. We establish and have a bottom line, a no-exception *policy* about how much we will put up with from others or how far they can go with us. This may mean getting as far away as possible if a dialogue cannot ensue.

Here is a more subtle example: A partner who says to us, "You are not enough," may be saying that he is seeking more from us than the 25 percent appropriate dose of need-fulfillment any one adult can expect from another. If he is narcissistic, he may mean that his entitlements are not being met. It is up to us to *ask what he means* exactly and to decide what we are willing to give. This is one way that we establish boundaries. We are not yet truly ourselves as long as we are being defined by others' needs and demands.

We can *refuse to engage* with others when they are attached to their unwarranted assumptions about us and refuse to open a dialogue with us.

We do not have to take the projections of others personally. We can *show compassion* for the pain behind a transference, the pain of unfinished business from a distressing past now foisted onto our relationship. Once we see that it happens compulsively and unconsciously, our compassion grows while we nonetheless continue to protect our own boundaries.

We can *simply notice* negative reactions from others without letting them stop or drive us into countertransference reactions. We are stopped when our self-esteem suffers by how they may have hurt us. We are driven if we have to run, appease, or retaliate. We can also notice positive reactions with a thank-you and appreciation. We are stopped when we become

caught in flattery and self-importance. We are driven when we use the respect others have for us to manipulate them in some way.

Spiritually, we may notice two results of our practices:

1. We foster a witnessing ego rather than a competitive one. This
   happens as a result of mindfulness meditation. *Then, giving up
   being an ego contestant in a relationship becomes more valuable
   to us than getting our way.*
2. We reduce the ego-emotional charge in how we respond to others.
   This happens as a result of loving-kindness practice. Then we say
   yes to the fact that there will always be some people who may not
   like us or who may react negatively to us. Then we invest our energy into accepting that given, rather than into redesigning ourselves to reverse it.

As we maintain our boundaries more and more, we notice that we
grow in self-esteem and we no longer fear or become upset by situations
or people quite so much. As we grow in psychological sophistication, we
notice what others do without surprise. As we advance in spiritual consciousness, we notice without blame.

> *The danger of the transference states is the possibility of the patient
> misunderstanding them and taking them for fresh experiences instead
> of reflections from the past.*
> —Sigmund Freud

5

How Our Fears Figure In

*Transference-like expectations and fears are ubiquitous in daily life,
and all actions are influenced to a degree by hopes carried forward
from the archaic past.*
— Ernest Wolf, *Treating the Self*

Fears figure into the experience of transference. We often transfer because some past issues are still too threatening to face. It may be difficult to look directly at a wife who scares us as a Medusa mother did. Transference fears huddle in our relationships, often without notice or name, but they do not have to stay hidden.

At the beginning of his autobiography, the British philosopher Thomas Hobbes reports that his mother gave birth to twins: "Thomas" and "Fear." Many of us can relate to that statement. We feel fear daily. For many of us it may be an almost constant companion. Something happens and we immediately imagine that the worst will certainly follow. We then either become passive or we overreact. Our minds often fail to notice alternatives, but rather keep coming up with reasons to fear even more. Fear is often a failure of imagination, a loss of that most self-expansive of all our gifts.

Yet, we can trust the possibility of love and courage by recalling times when we did act in just those ways. We can picture the times when our peers or heroes acted that way and we can say, "I can do that too," or even "May their example help me be strong too." This is why we have saints and heroes. They speak to us from the human collective and encourage

83

us to find our full potential for virtue and courage. In the film *Brave-heart,* we were shown the Scottish hero William Wallace riding back and forth in front of his hesitant troops, encouraging them to fight bravely for freedom. That horse and rider are in us. Our heart, no matter how timid before the battle begins, can become "Braveheart" in the midst of it. As humans we are interconnected in every way. We do not automatically act bravely; we need encouragement, like the troops in the film. We often require a validation of our courage before it can be activated.

The encouragement was supposed to begin in childhood. Childhood wounds mostly refer to failures of our parents in granting us that support. What results is an ongoing struggle between the part of us that loves and the part of us that fears, the seesaw of our psychic life. That struggle enacts itself in relationships. It may be reminiscent of the way in which our parents alternately encouraged us at times and shamed us at others—with the resultant waffling in us between loving them and fearing them.

We are a chambered nautilus, not a butterfly. Early-childhood layers of irrational fear and fixation do not go away; we simply pile new layers on top of them. Fear and needy craving become habits and they hang on long after there is anything to be afraid of or anything for which to yearn. We may even conquer fear in some ways, yet continue to believe we are at its mercy. We still try to head off surprises or scary challenges, even when we have built enough resources to handle them.

Irrational fear and addictive fixation are also associated with delusion, since we may fear what is not truly threatening or desire what we do not really need. For example, we may be fearing rejection because of the isolation into which it thrusts us. Now, as adults, we have built up a reliable support system and yet we still fear rejection by some powerful—that is, transference-laden—individual in our lives. We also often fear a cause when a consequence can no longer happen. For instance, we may fear abandonment by a partner when a consequence that is applicable only to infants, death by desertion, is no longer possible.

Four Fearsome Hurdles

There are four tensions that impact all of us. Each is a given of life and a core issue in relationship. Each evokes fear and is a focus of transference. Each originates in our past and moves itself into the present. We cannot eliminate these four hurdles but we can learn to scale them with equanimity.

1. Comings and goings
2. Giving and receiving
3. Being accepted and being rejected
4. Letting go and moving on

Each of these elicits primitive needs, beliefs, feelings, expectations, and reactions—the building blocks of transference. All four become nodes of anxiety throughout our life cycle, because of their connection to our survival and because most of us do not trust our ability to deal with them. For instance, leavetakings by others, no matter how innocent, may feel like rejection and abandonment. It may be harder for some of us to be given to than to give. We may feel more threatened by being accepted lovingly than by being rejected.

Our sense of agency—otherwise known as personal power—was meant to develop in our toddler days by the encouragement that came from acceptance and acknowledgment by our parents. "Meant to" is a phrase used often in this book. It implies that something is part of normal development, instinctively necessary to growth, as in this example: tomato plants are meant to be in the sun. "Meant to" also points to a purpose—for example, school is meant to help us learn. We might combine these meanings and say that since we were meant for love, we require a setting meant to teach us how.

The less trustworthy our world was in childhood, the more complicated are our relationships later. For instance, a mother who frequently disappeared for a few days while she was out drinking does not give a child a sense of safety and reliability. Thus the comings and goings of later partners will have a more intense impact on that person than on those whose mothers were present every day of every year.

The four tensions that so often scare us can also be used as defenses or weapons. We might leave as a way of avoiding, escaping, or punishing. We might give as a way of creating dependency on us. We might let go as a way of abandoning our responsibility. The ego can use any human event to satisfy its own desires or to coddle its own fears. It is up to us to keep tabs on our choices and to look into our motivations. This is part of processing life experiences, which is what we are learning in this book.

We try to control these four pairs of possibilities, a sign that we doubt our ability to live through them once they occur. We have nothing to be ashamed of in that doubt; it is part of being human. But control is impossible in the face of these tensions; they can only be entered with an attitude of "Yes, now what?"

The four conflict areas of life, the four hurdles to human development, become the sources of so many of our problems and transferences. Following are a few examples:

COMINGS AND GOINGS

Comings may bring up fear of the challenge in something new or fear of the loss of old comforts. We may feel threatened at meeting new people. Goings may bring up a fear of abandonment or a sense of being cast adrift, terrifying prospects when so much of what our life is about is tied to other people.

Sensitive people are more apt to notice the subtle forms of closeness and distance in a partner's behavior. For instance, "Last year he sent me a birthday card with a personal note; this year he sent a standard card with no note." Such changes are felt as forms of going just as much as actual departures. It certainly hurts to be that sensitive, but nonetheless, we would never want to lose our sensitivity, only manage it.

Our fear of one more betrayal or one more failed connection may be what we are attempting to stave off by our expectations that others never leave us. Our transference keeps us locked in the vault of our past, in which goings led to disappointment and arrivals signaled danger. The coming of little brother may have meant less of the five A's for us. The goings of older brother may have meant less fun at home.

Our own arrivals may be sources of stress if we bring an expectation of how people are supposed to greet us. For instance, when we visited Grandma in childhood, she made a fuss over us and showed obvious exuberance about seeing us again. Now when we come back to a place after a long absence, we feel disappointed or hurt when our friends do not greet us with similar excitement or make a fuss over us. We are transferring onto them the face of someone from the past and expecting them to act as she did. In reality, we are feeling two levels of grief: we miss Grandma's special love, and we feel a lack of love from friends today. They add up to a single grief—the loss of a cherished way of being loved. Since our transferred expectation is so great, we unfortunately do not notice that they love us in their own, more adult way, not as an old woman did in 1944.

I noticed recently in my own life a clue to some tension I feel in comings and goings, though my mind tells me they are nothing to be afraid of. When I arrive or leave a place or when others arrive at my home or leave, I automatically say something funny without planning it. I do not have that skill ordinarily. Humor is a common way of releasing tension or lessening anxiety. If someone were to ask me if I were tense, I would honestly say no, but apparently my always accurate body is saying otherwise.

Places associated with comings and goings are usually stressful. There will always be more tension in a railroad station than in a restaurant. Events associated with comings and goings, such as a new boss or the end of a work project, may evoke anxiety. Once we simply notice the fact that comings and goings are apt to scare us in some way, we may gradually get a handle on how to breathe through them and not upbraid ourselves for our uneasiness. Breathing is a living symbol/reminder of how we continually let in what comes and release what is ready to go.

We are reactive not only to the comings and goings of others but also to the comings and goings of ourselves. Comings and goings become personal concerns when they take the form of staying put or moving on or out.

Goings also include goodbyes when a relationship does not work and is going nowhere. The goodbye of going might be scary to say, since to do so means to get on with one's life, a challenge that may be more daunting than staying in an unsatisfactory status quo. We also resist the completion that comes to us with a goodbye, because it evokes grief that may be hard to handle. Yet those feelings open an energy that leads to more ease in facing the challenge of change. How ironic that we fear the very thing that leads to liberation.

In a wider context, comings refer to births and goings to death. Our own birth was a going from the safety of the womb and a coming into a challenging world. Our death is a going from all the world has meant to us into nothingness or into a new kind of existence. We usually greet births with joy and mourn deaths. Both are natural events and therefore givens to be met with our unconditional yes. Birth is a new connection. Death is the end of a connection. Yet, though there are vultures waiting for our bones, we can still discern an exaltation of larks around us, at birth, during a lifetime, and at death.

The loss of connection when death threatens can be a great moment in our lives that releases us from our habitual inhibitions. If we know someone is suffering from a cancer that is not responsive to treatment, we automatically show more physical affection and speak more lovingly to her. We might have been reserved about hugging or even about sounding sentimental when she was healthy. Now we do both without embarrassment. Goings can open and soften us.

GIVING AND RECEIVING

Love is giving and receiving the five A's: attention, acceptance, appreciation, affection, and allowing. We say and believe we want to be loved, but it takes courage and skill to be loved by someone. It takes openness to receiving, and that can be scary if we have to be in control of all that happens. We may sense a demand that we give in return, even if that was not intended by the other person. We may be afraid that we will have to be committed and thereby lose our liberty or our hold on the reins of power.

The heart contains two atriums in the upper position and two ventricles in the lower position. The physical heart is a metaphor for our emotional life. Deep in our hearts we carry ventricles (openings) seeking closeness and love. But sitting on top of them are the atriums (chambers/vaults) of fears and defenses. We all contain both, but as our self-trust/self-esteem grows, we learn to manage these defenses so that they help us achieve intimacy and handle disappointment.

When we are disappointed or feel shortchanged because we did not receive all that we wanted from someone, emotionally or even financially, we discover a clue to our transference regarding receiving what we believe we deserve.

"I am supposed to get it all" sounds like the statement of a person with high self-esteem, though it could be a clue to neediness and self-doubt. This carries over into transference as an unreasonable expectation of partners or friends. If they fail to meet our expectations, we might feel justified in becoming demanding, petulant, or even retaliatory. We might forget that intimacy flourishes in an atmosphere of mended failures rather than in one of grievances and grudges.

Alternatively, the governing principle of our life might be "I am only worthy to get some of what I need" or "I always deserve less than others." That might be the result of not being given what we needed emotionally or noticing that our siblings were getting what we were being denied. We might also have been taught to *want* less than we need, so now it is hard to know what we want or need. How ironic this is, since spiritual teachers throughout the ages have assured us that all we can safely want is not more than we have and not to be attached to what we do have.

Finally, giving and receiving bring up the issue of money. We may be afraid to give money away or to spend it. We may be uncomfortable about receiving money as a gift or a loan. We may compulsively or uncontrollably spend or waste money. We may save more than we will ever need. Our personal style with money may elude our understanding: "I have so little, why do I spend and borrow so much?" Our way of handling money usually reflects back on how one or both of our parents handled it. Transference issues certainly reach into the purse. Parents who showed love by giving us things may have set up a transference that now explains our strong need to receive money, gifts, or special deals. Parents who were emotionally or financially withholding may have set up a transference that explains our compulsive need to hoard money—or food or things. As we work on our transferences, we clear ourselves of our infections by the past and become immune to it. We might then be surprised at what we do with our money once we are left to our own devices. We might also see how our money issues have affected our way of showing or fearing intimacy, since that too is about giving and receiving.

BEING ACCEPTED AND BEING REJECTED

This pair is about being liked/disliked, loved/hated, let in/pushed away. We do not experience these options on an individual level only. At the ancestral level, being ignored is not just being disregarded. It registers in our still-ancient psyche as a dreaded loss of the connection so necessary to survival in a world in which cooperation and belonging made for safety. A rejection or abandonment feels dangerous now because it still seems to threaten survival. We find it terrifying to imagine facing life alone, as if that were the equivalent of death. This may make us miss out on a rich possibility for self-knowledge, which happens in solitude in ways that cannot quite occur in rooms that are crowded with others, especially when they are holding us.

In addition, not getting what we want is often just what leads to a whole new chapter in our life. An abandonment by one partner may lead to meeting another who is more trustworthy. Hard luck can lead to good luck. In that combination of opposites is synchronicity, a meaningful coincidence, that escorts us to our destiny, sometimes through a vale of tears.

In any case, when someone leaves us in our life here and now, the continuing interchanges and attunements on which we thrive come to an abrupt halt. Our identity has now entirely gelled in the other person's mind with no further chance for input from us. This is another reason that an abandonment hits us with such a thud. The disengagement results in our image becoming frozen in the latest form in which it occurred to the other person. In effect, we can no longer reestablish a sense of who we are to each other. Abandonment places an embargo on growing, a frightening option for beings who flourish by evolving.

Abandonment may happen as indifference, a disengagement of one partner from the arguments and dramatic expression of feelings that were so lively in the relationship before. The other partner may interpret the new tranquility as a sign that things are getting better, when actually the bond is dying off. When one partner loses interest in the couple's journey or no longer cares how or if it continues, the story is nearing its end. Someone has to address what is happening if there is to be a chance for restoration.

A person may break up with us and then act as if we never had a relationship at all or that it was not as important as he had made it seem originally. He may not validate our own sense of loss or even acknowledge our presence in public at all. That hurts. As we mature in our spiritual practice of letting go of ego, we might no longer say, "How dare he treat me as if I were unimportant?" Instead, we handle our anger and grief on our own. And, finally, we might say, "How can I use this experience as part of the necessary dismantling of my entitled ego?"

Our ego is less neurotic when it accepts its provisional status in a world in which one of the givens is that we will not matter much to some people. The ego wants to force others to see our value or else to retaliate against them for not being willing to honor it. To let go is to move on. This means a combination of an unconditional yes to the way people are, without blame or revenge, and a greater carefulness about whom we trust in future relationships. "Why are people like this?" leads to blame. "Yes, some people are like this and now what?" leads to acceptance of a given, an opportunity for compassion, and a boost to moving on.

Being accepted includes a reliable sense that we are known and welcomed. Here is an example of how something can happen that seems superficial but picks up other meanings in our body-minds. I found myself feeling upset at the bank while cashing a check because the teller asked for two forms of identification. Later, I wondered why I reacted with so much disgruntlement, and soon I realized it was my sense of being a stranger to the bank staff, though in reality they knew me by name. I therefore expected them to make an exception for me, to exempt me from the standard policy. The bank was supposed to be a holding environment, like that of childhood, in which allowances were so often made for little David. My anger was not due to the fact that I was asked for double identification but rather to the thought that I was not loved. *Am I that needy?*

LETTING GO AND MOVING ON

To let go and move on in life can feel like a loss of connection as well as a loss of what comforts us. To let go is to lose our sense of control of an outcome, a scary possibility to those who still feel driven to make a plan and see that it is completed as they wanted it to be, irrespective of the unruly given that life is unpredictable. We may feel panic in an atmosphere in which the chips can fall anywhere they may.

We grow as we embark on our own heroic journey, the archetype of letting go and going on. Since it is an archetype, it is an innate, ancestral, positive urge, though also one that fear can override. At the same time, since the heroic journey is so crucial to the evolution of ourselves and of our planet, it presents us with just the grace we need to travel it. Evolution is the gradual decline of the ego's empire in favor of the kingdom of the higher Self, i.e., a progression from egocentricity to universal love. But we may sometimes find it hard to trust that, given our background.

Our hesitancy about moving on is not a sign of inadequacy. Something inside us wants to stay put, while something wants to go too. For some of us the householder-hearth archetype is more in evidence than the heroic-journey archetype. We may not have confronted that inclination in ourselves. The challenge is to balance both the traveling-hero and the stable-householder archetypes by allowing ourselves to move or stay as necessary. We recall that some birds migrate and some stay put, as Emily Dickinson describes in these stanzas:

> The Southern Custom—of the Bird—
> That ere the Frosts are due—
> Accepts a better Latitude—
> We—are the Birds—that stay.
>
> The Shiverers round Farmers' doors—
> For whose reluctant Crumb—
> We stipulate—till pitying Snows
> Persuade our Feathers Home.

Practice
Scaling the Hurdles with Grace

COMINGS AND GOINGS

This practice involves saying an unconditional yes to the given of comings and goings of others into and from our lives. We pronounce this yes by accepting and welcoming new challenges and letting go of what is ready to disappear. Rituals of welcome and of goodbye help us. We can devise them with any friends who join us in our challenges and losses. We can also settle into the reality that survival in this day and age means making new friends more easily and saying goodbye more easily too. This is the best way to handle the revolving door of change in people's choices to enter or leave our lives.

In the face of fear we might therefore be bold enough *to trade in our habits for practices* by affirming: "There is a trustworthy, ineradicable urge in me to let in new possibilities and it is fearless. I override the habit to be caught in my familiar comforts and open myself to what wants to come in. I align myself to reality rather than attempt to redesign it to appease the status quo. I watch comfortably as things pass away, knowing that is the nature of our transitory reality. I accept the fact of impermanence by reminding myself of my mortality, my own final going."

GIVING AND RECEIVING

We explore whether we were given what we needed in childhood. We recall birthdays and Christmases and ask ourselves how we felt. Do we still believe something is owed to us? The signal of this might be the belief now that it is all right to take what is not given to us. Do we believe, on the other hand, that we owe somebody something? The signal of this is the sense that we can never give enough.

Gradually, as we become more conscious, we move into the pure adult present where not all will be given and not all will be received *and* we can still survive. That "and" is our equanimity. By it we let others off the hook and act in accord with the givens of others' limitations. Equanimity is not insensitive distancing or cold neutrality. It is rather an embrace of experience without the mind-sets of "grab if pleasant" or "run if unpleasant." Instead, all conditions are held with equal composure.

With this virtue we are liberated from the transference style of using others to compensate for the limitations of our parents. In the generous forgiveness that follows, we let go of blaming them or anyone who does not come through for us. We do this because we are forgiving people who have settled something, not because we are victims who want to be nice at any cost. Strength is the ability to give and forgive without losing ourselves in the process.

BEING ACCEPTED AND BEING REJECTED

Here is a personal example of rejection and its connection to the past and to transference: From time to time in my life a friend will stop calling, and when I call or e-mail, he or she doesn't reply. This kind of sudden silence has hurt and bothered me all my life, and I never knew why (the reasons remained unconscious). Recently, a friend suddenly stopped communicating with me for no apparent or stated reason. I did what I usually do, trying to contact him by e-mail and by phone, but there was no reply and no explanation. This time I asked myself, "David, when did *sudden silence* first happen to you?" The answer came quickly, like a shock: Dad's sudden disappearance when I was two. Suddenly, it became clear to me why I was so bereft at the silence of my friend. In addition, this friend was also a father figure to me, so it resonated even more trenchantly.

My response was to notice and *feel* my feelings, say *yes* to his silence, *respect* his decision not to let me know why he did not want contact. I decided to *accept* my not-knowing and look again at my own *grief* about Dad's disappearance. That new focus turns the attention to my own work on myself and I can *learn* from my experience. Finally, in accord with loving-kindness I made a promise to myself never to use the sudden-silence treatment on others. Then others do not have to suffer as I did.

LETTING GO AND MOVING ON

We take an inventory of how we are stuck, how we move too slowly or too fast, how we procrastinate. We look at our fears of moving on. We ask what we are holding on to and then look at our fears of letting go.

We have it in us to transcend the fear of seeing what we are really about and of getting on with life in new ways. When we notice that we are afraid and are trying to remain in control, we can use the following practice:

Picture yourself holding the fear of what *might happen* in one hand. In the other, hold what you plan to control and *make happen*. Between your hands is the real you that says yes to *whatever happens*.

Letting go is tossing away our pennant of control. The ego uses control to mask its fear or run from it. Pure fear feels like powerlessness. The path to liberation from fear is, paradoxically, not to get back in control but to enter into the space around and in our helplessness and thereby to feel it fully. This is how we let go of the illusion of control and open to a new kind of power in ourselves, the power to face and handle what life brings, the essence of fearlessness.

Success at letting go of fear in even very small ways shows us there is a limit to how far our fear can escalate. We also notice that there is a limit to how much it can disempower us, another encouraging realization. This was known to the ancients, since the *Bhagavad Gita* says, "Even a little progress is freedom from fear."

> *The path of integration does not flee anxiety but endures it, in order to recuperate those parts of the psyche which split off and returned to haunt us in projected symbolic form.*
> —David Loy

6

Our Compulsion to Repeat

*This way of seeing removes the burden from the early years as having
been a mistake and yourself a victim of handicaps and cruelties; instead it is the acorn in the mirror, the soul endlessly repeating in different guises the pattern of your Karma.*
                                                    —James Hillman

Repetition helps us get through things. The repetition of the story of a
personal tragedy helps reduce the stressful impact so it can settle in us as
a fact we can live with. The repetition of a positive event makes it possible to reexperience the joy and be comforted by it.

We repeat in relationships what happened in childhood not because
there is something wrong with us. Repetition helps us resolve the past,
but only if we are so conscious of it that we can process it and let it go.
Often we simply repeat without getting to the next stage. So we use the
correct method (repetition) but not with the correct follow-up (resolution). In this chapter we explore all this and find a way to use repetition
as a bridge into resolving our past.

We notice repetition everywhere. Repetition is repeated evidence that
something is incomplete. We do not find repose in any venture until we
gain a sense of satisfactory completion, be it emotionally or physically. If
we hear part of a song, we tend to finish it in our heads. We feel at a loss
when someone dies before we had our chance to say goodbye, to clear up

our disputes, to make our amends. Without completion we might "curse the scanty love we were content to show," as Emily Dickinson wrote so movingly in a poem about how we feel after the loss of a loved one ("We cover thee, sweet face").

We notice that nature operates by repetition: dawn and dusk, moon cycles, orbits of planets, seasons. Our bodies also work by repetition: heartbeats, breaths, sleeping/waking. History repeats itself, for better or worse. It seems that repetition is built into life and reality, so it must have a useful purpose in our psychological life as well as in our evolutionary world.

Repetition is certainly a theme in Eastern religion. The notion of "karma" refers, among other things, to the tendency to repeat a past good deed or error. We strengthen the inclination to be kind when we choose to act with kindly love. We are more likely to do further harm after we have chosen to hurt someone. Karma is about repetition as a virtue or a danger.

Nietzsche wrote of "the eternal return" and declared that "the merely going round is an ultimate good." His definition of a hero is, in fact, "he that is strongly a master of repetition." We recall that there are two ways of going around: The spiral is positive repetition, ever-evolving in an upward trend. The spinning wheel in the snow is the negative repetition, ever wasting energy.

The Russian psychologist Bluma Zeigarnik identified the "Zeigarnik effect" in 1927. She demonstrated that incomplete tasks are retained in our memories much longer than completed ones. This accounts for our tendency to hold on to negative or defect-revealing memories longer than positive ones.

Interruptions and foreshortenings make a lasting impression and demand a conclusion. This is an ancient realization. Saint Paul sees the yearning for completion as a quality of nature: "All creation groans as in the pangs of childbirth even until now" (Rom. 8:22). Carpocrates, a Neoplatonist of the second century, proposed that the soul must repeat the whole gamut of human experiences if it is ever to be free of the body once and for all. Belief in the necessity of repetitions by reincarnation has this same ring.

Speaking philosophically, we can say that built into every living thing, humans included, is an autopoiesis, a "self"-making tendency, as the

Greek-based word denotes (also giving us the word *poetry*). Autopoiesis
is the inner drive in something to become itself and instinctively to act
in ways that foster its own self-realization. Autopoiesis helps us understand our drive toward completion and the repetition it may take to accomplish it. We might say that it is a positive compulsion. We cannot do
otherwise than self-realize unless we consciously override this natural
proclivity by stunting ourselves through, for example, the use of addictive substances or staying too long in relationships or situations that hurt
or hobble us.

Our full humanity is not only achieved by becoming physically and
psychologically healthy but also by becoming enlightened and loving
persons. This means that there is a natural predisposition in us toward
repeated expressions of virtue, toward Buddha mind, toward Christ consciousness. The love and wisdom in those archetypes are not alien to us
but represent our own innate potentials yearning to be expressed. Our
ego wants to reach its highest potential for awareness, wisdom, and compassion. Only then is it finally at rest in fulfilling the purpose for which
it seems to have been designed: not the myopic egotism of "only-I" but
the empathic, interconnected consciousness of "I-you."

Autopoiesis happens best when our heart responds rather than our
head takes control, when our soul moves us rather than rules and concepts. Notice that Pinocchio in the Disney cartoon learns that he can become real if he follows the rules. He is also easily prey to the temptation
to grow by joining the circus. Yet his realness can only truly happen when
he risks his life for others. His heart responded and his soul opened with
courage. Only then was the blessing of realness bestowed.

Spiritual practices are repetitions and certainly technologies of autopoiesis. For instance, when we practice mindfulness in relationships,
we are not forcing ourselves to be what we are not. Rather we are *aligning* our behavior to who we really are in any given moment. We are not
rubbing against the grain when we practice loving-kindness; we are
going with the grain of love and kindness that underlies, animates, and
accounts for our existence. In our deepest being, we *want* to love everyone, because our deepest being *is* love. There is a Neoplatonic concept
that goodness can't help but spread itself around and thereby expand.
Shakespeare knew this too, as when Juliet says to Romeo:

"My bounty is as boundless as the sea,
My love as deep; the more I give to thee,
The more I have, for both are infinite."

Events Too Huge

Some of us want to revisit the past; some of us want to reverse it; some of us want to repeat it. Most of us engage in all three in the course of life. We often resist the completion of an experience or relationship, preferring to repeat what we do not complete. Unconscious transference is one way we repeat. This is the opposite of addressing, processing, resolving, and integrating our experiences.

We may unconsciously be seeking a partner who will repeat the nonfulfillment of our needs, just as happened in childhood. This may happen in one relationship after another. Ironically, we may associate repetition with safety.

Important things impact us in layers. This is what is meant by "depth" rather than "superficiality" in our experience. The depth-layerings of events may also explain rituals of repetition, of which transference is one. Transference, like a recurrent dream, keeps happening until and so that the underlying tension it addresses can be resolved. Repetition attenuates and titrates the painful impact of a traumatic event so that it does not assault us all at once. The repetition becomes a compulsion when we fixate on it or are frustrated in our attempts to find satisfaction of it. We are impassioned with a relentless desire to heal any needed union that has been damaged. Satisfaction happens in completion. Why is this?

In transference we attempt to complete with new people what is still incomplete with the original people. Transference is, in that way, a technology of autopoiesis, of self-creation. By transference we open the healthy possibility of self-completion. By keeping it unconscious we curtail its benefits; by making it conscious we capitalize on them.

On a larger scale, we notice what Rilke wrote to a young poet: "Have patience with everything unresolved and try to love the questions." Some events are so enormous or have such deeply archetypal implications that they will have to be repeated forever without any final completion, at least not in any one lifetime.

Positive examples of this need to repeat without end are found in the perennial restaging of famous plays. They are presented over and over throughout the centuries because the human mind will never be able to let in their message fully: A son kills his father and marries his mother (*Oedipus Rex*); a prince finds out his father was murdered and is commanded to take revenge (*Hamlet*). We will understand the plots, but we will never fully know Oedipus or Hamlet, their motivations, their secret desires—just as we did not fully know our own father's or our son's motivations or desires. We watch the plays again and again, as if drawn to a mystery that we know is crucial to our personal development yet cannot be grasped in any full or final way. This happens because we are beholding our own story, a piece at a time, in theirs. Thus, in each succeeding stage of our own life we are able to feel more intensely and understand more deeply the plots and characters in Shakespeare. When we are in college, *King Lear* presses into us only in a minor way, whereas in later life, it pierces us like a harpoon. We see our own archaic scenarios played out in the play, in different roles each time, hoping to gain at least some understanding of what is ultimately too overwhelming for hearts like ours to plumb.

How can we believe our family put us in such predicaments as they did? How can we believe humans do the things we see happening on the bloody stage? How can we believe such ingratitude is possible from those for whom we have done so much?

A positive example of repeating in order to absorb a little more each time, but never totally, is our participation in religious rituals. How could we ever grasp fully a miraculous release from slavery? So the feast of Passover has to be repeated till the end of time. It will take that long for the human psyche to let in the enormity of the gift of Exodus. How could we ever grasp fully that the body and blood of God has been given to us as spiritual food? The innumerable daily Masses throughout the world do not begin to exhaust the mystery fully. Great gifts, like great events, require an eternity to assimilate. Perhaps belief in eternity arose from just such a realization.

In the religious realm, repetition is a powerful tool of self-discovery. People are called to repeat the practices of, and pattern their behavior after, those of saints and sages. Indeed, rituals become most meaningful when they are forms of imitation of divine gestures. Grace is received because of ritual imitation, a repetition of spiritual events—for example, Passover, Eucharist. Thus, repetition has indelible and unmistakable meaning in the deep structures of the collective human psyche. Repetition is not simply doing what was done before; it is an initiation into the grace of primal events and a path to spiritual self-realization.

Negative events, like the Holocaust, have to be recalled frequently, since the human heart can never fully grasp that it is capable of such horrors. In addition, we recall how our country came into our hands because of the greed and genocide of our ancestors. We are disturbed to see modern presidents repeating the cycles of war, and we wonder when we humans will be committed to the survival of the planet through the arts of peace. Grief-striking events like these include repeatedly telling the story of what happened and standing up for a new political style of justice through nonviolence. This is how the need to repeat facilitates our ability to live with the collective shadow of humanity. We are never released from our shadow fully, and nonetheless we never cease working for change.

Something Ancient and Primitive Within Us

While writing this book, I dreamed I was telling my father's father that I sometimes miss Dad, who died many years ago. Grandpa answered that he missed him too. "When I miss him," he said, "I go down to the room where he was born and simply sit." This dream helped me understand more about transference, and mindfulness too. I speak of my ongoing relationship to Dad, though he is gone. I speak to Grandpa, also gone. He tells me he goes into the unconscious ("I go down"), where he contacts origins ("where he was born"). Transference is precisely about making that connection. We find our original issues in the unconscious and visit them when we feel incomplete. Then we "simply sit"—that is, in mindful awareness. I feel this dream is also a boon in the sense that past generations are helping me write these pages. Indeed, transference is generational karma: events with some people lead to a reprise of events with other people.

Freud explained that we are often not trying to "find an object in real perception . . . but to refind such an object, to convince oneself that it is still there." Is this what transference is about, trying to convince myself that the past is still there, Dad still being born in the room downstairs, the depths of my soul and simultaneously this room where I now stand? Is this how I attempt to begin our relationship again?

As we saw earlier, we feel things at a personal level but also at village, ancestral, tribal, and collective levels. All those levels still reside in our bodies, the most local version of the unconscious. We have a long archetypal memory, like cats. Some say that the reason cats are careful in approaching us is that their bodies recall the abuse they suffered in the course of history from us humans. Dogs have a short archetypal memory, so they jump into our arms without hesitation, for better or for worse.

An example of our clan memory is in the sense that something good we have just been granted will surely be taken back. This is not traceable only to early childhood but is a common human fear, based on a sense of unworthiness and a need for constant humility in order to be pleasing to the lords and masters who tolerate and permit our existence. Deep down—which here means at the level of our tribal mentality—we might still believe that we are never truly deserving and that we are lucky when our happiness lasts or when a needed partner still stays. *Or is it only Romeo who will say, "I still will stay with thee," not anyone I will meet?*

We can practice attentiveness to our primitive reactions to the events or crises in our daily life. Even if they seem minor, they may have weight and magnitude. We see an example of this in physical trauma. A fall from a motorcycle may seem like a minor accident, but its impact on our body may be heavier than our mental description—or dimissal—of it. Likewise, childhood psychological events sound now as if they were not so major, but that does not mean that they were not felt to be overwhelming when they happened. Most primal experiences were accompanied by long-lasting cellular reactions over which we have no control and of which we may be ignorant. This may be hard to believe, since our ego's sense of control is insulted by the fact that our unconscious is more in charge than we are. Yet, the body cannot be talked out of its original pang and its lingering clang.

Why We Are All So Concerned about Abandonment

I arrive at the airport and wait for the friend who has agreed to pick me up. It becomes quite late and he has not shown up. I call his number, but there is no answer. I have no cell phone, so he cannot contact me. My intellect may infer simply, and probably accurately, that something has gone awry, something beyond his control. That is my adult mind speaking. But, at the same time, I begin to feel a gnawing sense of being deliberately disregarded and deserted. That is my primitive body-mind speaking. It lectures more loudly in places of comings and goings, such as airports. This is because comings and goings hit us where we are most vulnerable, in the realm of connections (because of which we survive) or broken connections (because of which we break down). My sense of being marooned is a thus a "village reaction" from a collective reminiscence.

Now I am feeling something that is no longer simply about a friend's tardiness. This is about the tardy disloyal love so reminiscent of the missed appearances of a whole parade of family members, friends, and lovers, of the rejections and excommunications pronounced upon me throughout all the decades of my life by people and institutions. I am still believing that these abandonments happened because of my unworthiness, and that is how I imagine this absent friend to be sizing me up today. So I stand here waiting, when really I am bent over with griefs that were waiting for me from eras long past. How can I still believe there is such a thing as "past"?

This event can, however, certainly become a source of personal growth. I can talk to myself like a kindly uncle as I stand and wait: "A matter-of-fact error has occurred today, a given of the mishaps in life. Yet, I notice I am feeling it in a big way. I guess I still believe I am not really worthy of loyalty, and this event is triggering my old sense of inadequacy. I carry this belief now and I stand with it here in this moment of disappointment. This has alerted me to a rich theme to work on in my next therapy session, which needs to be soon. Meanwhile I am ready to let go of this 'village reaction' and take a cab."

Abandonment means being excluded, a crucial issue for primitive peoples. Our primitive feelings, as we just saw, have a collective dimension and are not under the control of our educated ego. Therapy and books like this one do not reach into that deep chasm, nor can it ever be emptied. We can help ourselves, as in the example above, by simply noticing that our personal feelings are picking up on collective ones, and we can simply let them be. Paradoxically, we can at least be comforted by the sense of kinship with others across the centuries who feel and felt what we are feeling now.

Abandonment fears thrive on a mistaken belief: "I will die if I am left alone." This fear is likely to arise when there is a combination of a trigger point, such as waiting for a delayed friend at the airport, and a low ebb in personal strength because of a recent crisis or stress. Then we are more likely to be catapulted into our primitive mode, which is never too far below the level of ordinary consciousness, and imagine the worst is happening. Perhaps crises are engineered by the psyche, which wants so much to have us work on ourselves so that we can finally be paroled from our past. In that sense, could it be that it is all synchronicity, the mysterious combination of chance and meaning?

We can understand our extreme and primitive reactions by using an analogy: The psyche is like a file cabinet belonging to someone with very few folders. She therefore has to place files in folders with very general rather than specific or exact titles. "Abandonment," for instance, is one title of a folder in the cabinet. "He didn't call back," "He didn't notice my new dress," "He didn't kiss me the way he used to," "He didn't come back home at all"—all these go into the same folder irrespective of their varying levels of importance. They hit with equal impact. Likewise, "father," "authority," "boss," "rules" might also go into one folder and thereby all read out as one. This tendency in the psyche for different things to blur into one thing certainly facilitates transference.

We emerged from childhood with few folders in our mental cabinet, since these folders were set up before we had the sophistication to realize that things that happen can have many subtle meanings. The appropriate titles of folders would in fact be the specific nuances of an experience. Yet, many experiences have a similar but not exactly the same nuance, as in the example above in which not noticing a new dress reads out to us as equal to being abandoned. It is up to us to expand our filing cabinet and make its folders more accurately reflective of the variety of human experiences. Our inner kindly uncle helps us in this: "So he didn't notice the dress. Chalk it up to his being distracted about his own problems, as people can be. This is not about you. File this under 'The Givens of Life: People are not loving all the time,' or the 'How Henry Is' file, not the one marked 'I've been Abandoned Again.'"

Abandonment is a collective theme. Why is the abandonment file so personally prominent? Adulthood is an extension of our childhood, not a replacement of it. The scared child still desperately seeks reassurance and gets rattled when someone refuses to return his calls. Even though that may not matter to the adult part of us, it does matter enormously to the child part of us, where feelings happen so powerfully, where any form of abandonment is terrifying because it picks up on past traumas or collective ones.

Our minds may minimize the legitimacy of our feelings, dubbing them irrational. We can offset this tendency by granting hospitality to the full spectrum of our feelings. Then they might take us by the hand back to events never processed or even yet recalled. To accept our feelings now is to accept the bereft-child part of us and hold him at last in ways he was not held when first he felt alone.

The Impact on Us

Here is another example of a primitive reaction and how it reveals transference: I am cut off in traffic. I take it as a personal insult. This highway event is not personal, however, since the other driver is cutting off a car, not a person. He is not doing it to insult *me* but to get to his own destination as quickly as he can, with little regard for courtesy. Personalizing is the sign of an unconscious transference. We become conscious of the transference and learn from it when we notice it and make our own psychotherapeutic intervention on ourselves: "This level of reaction shows me I am feeling something from my past that is unresolved. This is not about that driver and me."

Most of us can never fully imagine just how insulted we felt in childhood. Now, behind the wheel, we feel an insult as giant-size. In childhood, we took abuse or insult in stride and made excuses for our family members or blamed ourselves in order to reduce the wallop. As pain became familiar, it no longer registered as pain to us but as routine. Little bodies could not endure as much as our adult bodies can endure. Now in the car we can rage wildly, because it is all anonymous and we are ensconced in steel. We can now feel safely what we could not feel before. How much of our fury toward the other driver is really rageful grief for how cruel or disappointing our interfering mother was or how our baby sister's arrival in the family cut us off from so much of the affection to which we had become accustomed? Are we recalling someone else who cut off our "Whee!" with a "Whoa!"?

The challenge is to sustain our feelings rather than become possessed by them—that is, swept away by them, compelled to act them out inappropriately. This is the powerless-child set of reactions that lets feelings in and then jams them up in continual recycling.

Hate and Hurt

We can look at rage as an example of a feeling that recycles: hate and hurt *within a transference* can be part of a sad and painful cycle: hurt, hate, hurt. Someone has hurt us in the past. We hate him for it. We show our hate by hurting someone in the present who reminds us of him. But our hurting that person does not satisfy our rage, because we are hurting the wrong person. We are as upset and enraged as we are partly because what has hurt us in our present conflict recalls a hurt from the past from another person. We are trying to get back at a phantom through a live person now. So of course our hurt cannot be resolved, nor can our hate be dissipated.

We interrupt the cycle when we grieve the hurt rather than pass it on. This locates the issue in us rather than maintaining it as a transaction. Grief work leads to our letting go of resentment. *Since grief work leads to forgiveness, it is itself an act of love for others.* Thereafter we respond to those who hurt us not in the manner of the prize-fighter who damages his opponent. Our style, instead, is that of aikido, in which we work *with* someone's aggressive energy in nondamaging but nonetheless self-protective ways.

We might say that hate is rage with a blind, insatiable need for revenge. The insatiable quality gives us a clue that the anger is a repetition of transferences and projections that arose from ancient hurts. Healthy people do not hate, because they address and resolve painful feelings, which is the opposite of feeding the unquenchable need to continue punishing.

People with spiritual consciousness do not hate, because they are committed to loving-kindness. People who are psychologically healthy do not hate, but resolve issues rather than turn them into feuds. People who do hate deserve our compassion, not our retribution, because if the circumstances were extreme enough, we too would probably become as confused as the haters, and become enmeshed in the same self-defeating web of recycled retaliation.

Practice
Staying with Feeling

Healthy adults let feelings in and through. We simply stay with what we feel, and gradually a realization comes. Feelings teach. In relationship to the events of today, our feelings are the link to our past. We are then able to look at how our feelings connect to the past. By dealing with feelings as both real in the present and connected to the past, we gain double benefit. Our issues can reveal their roots to us when we take note of the transference dimension in them.

If we feel stuck in a certain emotional state or resistant to change, we practice simply staying with ourselves in our stuckness or resistance. We do this as we begin to trust the power of staying/sitting mindfully in our own reality no matter how uncomfortable or how seemingly useless.

We may then notice that nothing stays put for very long. We notice an automatic and gentle shift of some kind. Our stuckness opens in some way. We have stayed within the lap of our own truth, and it transformed into a new truth. To stay with our truth in a pause is to lean into it and, ironically, the leaning readies us for standing. To "stay with" becomes to "stand up."

To stay with a feeling becomes a comfort, because it is an assurance that we will not abandon ourselves. That commitment to ourselves becomes a kind of *protection*, because it is worth more than all our successes at escaping our feelings and eluding our own condition. Even staying with our doubt, despondency, and utter vulnerability makes them all legitimate landscapes of our psychic life.

Our practice is to hold and relate to our feelings as *teachings* about enlightenment. The teachings emerge both from what incites our feelings and from our ways of responding. Sadness teaches us about loss and impermanence. Anger shows us how we react to unfairness. Fear teaches us about how we handle danger and threat. Joy teaches us about how we celebrate life.

We stay with ourselves by giving ourselves the five A's: attention, acceptance, appreciation, affection, and allowing.

When such staying power is applied to another person, it is *commitment.*

This and all our work culminates in "yes." We say an unconditional yes to the given of life that our needs will not always be met and also to the first noble truth of Buddhism, that life includes unsatisfactoriness. When I say yes to these givens, I can free myself from inappropriate entitlement. I am then open to moments of satisfaction and can draw the curtain on lamenting past dissatisfaction. I simply stay in this moment, and the satisfaction that comes from not abandoning myself becomes more valuable than whether anyone is staying with me. This is the high road to liberation from the fear of abandonment.

The nurturing power in this loyalty to the moment is described so well in William Wordsworth's "Tintern Abbey":

> . . . *in this moment there is life and food*
> *for future years.*

Finally, regarding hate, we contact our hurt, and use our model of grief work, as in chapter 9. We commit ourselves to taking responsibility for our feelings by addressing, processing, resolving, and integrating them in accord with the practice in chapter 2.

In addition, we recall what the eighth-century Indian teacher Shantideva said in *The Way of the Bodhisattva:* "May those whose hell it is to hate and hurt be turned into lovers bringing flowers." As we recite this aspiration, we can feel the power of loving-kindness changing our attitude from retaliation to reconciliation, from hate to compassion. We rest serene as we trust the wisdom of the sages. Our ancestors have bequeathed us remedies, not only damages.

7

Memories of Mistreatment

In the earliest stage of life, it is possible for a child to forget about the extreme acts of cruelty he or she has endured and to idealize her perpetrator. But the nature of the subsequent enactment reveals that the whole history of early persecution was stored up somewhere . . . . In psychoanalytic treatment, the story is enacted within the framework of transference and counter-transference.
—Alice Miller, *For Your Own Good*

Someone snarls at us and we hear only our drunken dad's sarcasm from long ago. A parent may have severely scared us and we carry that inner fear around with us, looking for a place to drop it off. Yet we cannot succeed in transferring what is deeply ours to someone else's territory.

Some of our unconscious memory is repressed; some of it is dissociated. Repressed memories are those that become deeply hidden in our unconscious because they are too threatening to face. Memories in early life that are too terrifying to recall may be repressed/forgotten for the sake of our own welfare. We are not ready or able to handle them, so the protective devices of the psyche keep them from us. In this regard, and throughout this book, our work on ourselves has to be respectful of the inner timing that protects our sensitive heart from facing too much too soon. This is not a sign of some deficiency. It is a respect for the wisdom of the psyche's schedule, which is more reliable than that of the ego, which may want to prove its muscle at the cost of readiness.

Dissociation is absenting ourselves from abuse while it is happening by taking refuge in alternative thoughts or images. For example, while a child is being sexually abused, she may dissociate from the event by imagining herself to be somewhere else—or even someone else. We dissociate so that we can distract ourselves from the pain or horror of what is happening to us. Dissociation is a more deliberate and immediate escape than forgetting an event later, as happens in repression.

Whether we recall abuse now or dissociated from it, we all contain an inner archetypal sense of what a good parent is. If a father was an alcoholic and beat us severely, we knew instinctively, though perhaps not consciously at the time, that this was wrong. Deep down, we knew that our parent was supposed to protect us. When mother was silent while we were being abused, we realized that something necessary for our survival was missing. Imagine how terrifying that was.

An abused child, in order not to feel like an orphan, may protect his parents by identifying with their negative belief about him. He interprets the mistreatment as his own fault and therefore as legitimate punishment. This keeps the idealized parents in their (undeserved) ideal state. *The psyche wants to experience connection more than it wants to recognize the presence of abuse.* The psychologist W. R. D. Fairbairn comments, "It is better to live as a sinner in a world created by God than to live in a world created by the devil."

In adulthood, we may unconsciously repeat our parents' behavior toward our spouse and children as a way of legitimizing our past and of making it more bearable to ourselves. We may misuse any power we have at work or in the world. Consciously, we may feel anger and indignation. The part of us that has colluded with our abusive parent against us remains firmly in our unconscious. We might then prolong the damage done to us by abusing others. We may engage in this compulsively, not quite knowing why, a clue to unconscious transference.

We might stay in relationships in which we are being mistreated. That can happen when the familiar is more valuable to us than an escape from it. When we are being abused in an adult relationship, we may feel powerless to change or escape. That powerlessness is a memory of the past, not an indication of who we are now. The work is to experience our feelings, and to work on them and their connection to the past to whatever extent we are ready. Only letting the light through can help us: making the unconscious conscious, the implicit explicit, the yet-unexposed exposed. Then the cell door opens of its own accord and we can finally get away from the abuse.

Some partners, even after we stand up to them, go on scaring us in inexplicable ways. We then have work to do in therapy together. When that is refused by our partner, we are ready to go away for a while or permanently. "But I love him" may make us stay where it keeps hurting. Since the connection between love and abuse happened in childhood when we could not leave home, we may still feel trapped and believe that love means staying with abusers. We may still believe the collective myth that it is acceptable for someone to love and hurt us at the same time. Love is then used to endorse abuse. The abused one believes her pain is an obligatory part of love, justified, to be borne rather than to be confronted, shunned, or fled from. Love means unconditional caring, but it does not mean remaining under the same roof with an abuser. Sometimes love can only happen from a distance.

When one parent is truly mean or malicious toward us, our transference may extend to everyone of the same gender. Our individual experience with mother may turn us against all women. This can be a source of misogyny in men or misanthropy in women. It can also make it difficult for a woman to trust other women or for a man to trust other men.

Our feeling of being scared or intimidated by someone, whether or not it is intended, can be confronted by the practice in chapter 2: addressing, processing, resolving, and integrating. We apply it to abuse when we *address* abuse by calling it by name and speaking up about it, placing it on the table so it can be dealt with. We *process* by showing our angry feelings and the full range of our grief and by acknowledging the transference dimension. We *resolve* the issue by seeing things change as the abuser seeks and uses therapeutic help. If this does not happen, we move on. We *integrate* the new awareness into our life by acting in new, stronger ways that do not permit abuse or intimidation and that set clear boundaries in future relationships in order to keep ourselves safe.

Unfortunately, fear of a partner in a relationship is often unnoticed, so it is not even addressed. It happens as an undertow more than as a tidal wave. Loyalty to the intimidating partner is then a compulsion, not a choice. Our secondary gain (which is a positive though unconscious benefit from a negative experience) is the sense of familiarity, often a comforting transference even if painful: "At least I feel I am at home and know the rules. I can't expect much more from life." In such despair, we are caught in the transference rather than being able to address and process it. We don't see an alternative, because familiarity blinds us to the possibility that we could receive the five A's rather than living with the fiery rage and the smoldering threat of abandonment that may have characterized our childhood.

The pervasive anxiety we feel, the eggshells we walk on, do not easily lead to resolution by connecting them with the past. We have first to work in therapy, or if that fails, to get away for a while from the one who scares us. Then we can look at our personal issues from the past and become hardier. If we later choose to, we can come back to face the one who scared us and report to him the full story of our pain.

For some of us, such matter-of-factness is the end of transference, and may mean the end of the excitement of the relationship, if that is all it ever really consisted of. This may be a clue to why so many of us do not step out. The combination of fear and desire, of pain and pleasure, the essence of melodrama, may be more animating or sustaining than liberation from it. This is how our encapsulation in our addiction to adrenaline is becomes so long-lasting.

Emily Dickinson warns us of the danger of such comforting imprisonment:

> *How soft this Prison is*
> *How sweet these sullen bars*
> *No Despot but the King of Down*
> *Invented this repose . . . .*
> *A Dungeon but a Kinsman is*
> *Incarceration—Home.*

Ongoing Stress

Memories last. That is a given of human life. But memories of abuse do not have to keep hurting us. We can address, process, resolve, and integrate them through our grief work. Our sad memories may then remain in us, but only as shrapnel that is too deep to be excised, but no longer harmful in any case.

However, childhood conflicts, as well as the painfully remembered ravages wrought by former relationships, may have left us war-torn, experiencing posttraumatic stress, and skittish about new partners. We may then carry wounds that keep reopening when the possibility of new love appears. We fear taking a chance. We find it difficult to trust others. We may exhibit symptoms of Posttraumatic Stress Disorder (PTSD), such as the following:

- Anxiety attacks with no obvious reason
- Ongoing and obsessive recalling of injury, either mental or cellular/ physical, often with flashbacks
- Expecting the worst to happen
- Having dreams or nightmares about the originally distressing experiences
- Behaving or feeling as if the primal traumas were happening in the present
- Feeling intense reactions to any events that symbolize or are reminiscent of what happened in the past
- Avoiding, numbing, denying, dissociating, or detaching from any person, place, or thing that resembles or revives the past trauma
- Becoming addicted to substances or behaviors or becoming obsessed with a person or belief—all of which serves as a distraction from grief

We can see how these same elements show up in our struggles in relationship. We may be plagued with memories of the insults to our human dignity by abusers. Such memories do not remain in our heads; they spill over into suspicions of partners who do anything at all that reminds us of our past, even unintentionally. The past keeps presenting its bill, but to the wrong debtor. We might dream of past difficult partners while sleeping next to a new partner; the proximity is more than a metaphor in our unconscious. As we saw above, our brain can confuse past and present, leading to intense and dramatic reactions to neutral events.

The issue in posttraumatic stress is that the past goes on hurting us and we feel that we are at its mercy. Working through the transference by which it is expressed can help us heal some of our wounds, though timing is essential in the process. As we saw above, we can only work on ourselves when the time is right. We know it is right when we are ready to take baby steps in that direction, no matter how awkward or embarrassing, no matter who is looking. The body seeks a homeostatic state; it looks for ways out of stresses that deplete or overtax it. So we are not alone in our baby steps. Just as when we learned to walk, there is support for our will to move.

Fear can induce us to despair that things can ever change. Often, our need to repeat an abusive or intimidating past is stronger than our need for a healthy relationship. This is positive in the sense that we believe in "first things first," that we are obliged to finish old business before we can approach our new business. We want to work through our old fears and then find healthy intimacy untrammeled by the past.

Our Delicate Timing

> *O time thou must untangle this, not I.*
> *It is too hard a knot for me to untie.*
> —Shakespeare, *Twelfth Night*

Both transference and its resolution involves returning to the past. The Greek word *nostos* means "return." The word for "pain" is *algos*. Together they form the English word *nostalgia,* which is a kind of homesickness for past experiences and connections. We long to go back, yet at the same time that longing also hurts. The word *nostopathy* means "pain upon coming back." It refers mainly to the pain felt by soldiers when they return home after a war. Now we understand this pain to be part of the posttraumatic stress described above.

The pain we may feel in our returns is part of the stress that is so common in comings and goings. In working with transference, we are attempting to go back to the reality of what happened to us in the past, and that is certainly painful. Memories we return to are often disturbing. Repetition of the past is likewise a painful revisiting. Both in the experience of transference and in dealing with it we see the connection between return/ repetition and pain.

One meaning of an algorithm is solving a mathematical problem by repeating an operation. Perhaps transferences are algorithms in human computations by which we repeat something until we feel it is solved. Some repetition is stuckness, a spinning of wheels. Some repetition happens because we are too flooded with emotions to come up with a creative response to the immediate problem. This is where timing has to be respected.

Rather than jump in and uncover the past too hastily, it is important to be compassionate toward ourselves by finding our own unique pace and taking in only as much as we can handle at any one time.

By means of synchronicity, relationships come along that present the next piece of some huge issue we have been carrying and carrying over, transferring it onto others. The universe seems to join us in our work and to honor our timing too. For instance, in our thirties we do some grief work about our abusive upbringing and then we come back to it in our forties from a different angle in a new relationship, job, or recent circumstance in our marriage. Then we might revisit it yet again in later life. *Each time the work is complete for the time being.* When we want to work on our transferences, we can trust that they will open to us at just the right time. "Hurry or delay are interferences," says British child psychiatrist D. W. Winnicott.

In a relationship, a feature of attention is to notice and honor a partner's resistance to addressing, processing, resolving, and integrating an issue that has arisen. Deep or persistent inquiry into issues and motivations will feel like intrusion to those of us with slower timing. If we are introverts, our timing is certainly different from that of most extroverts. Our readiness for intimacy is highly sensitive when we suffer from a fear of closeness. Our inner world remains our sacred space, with walls of safety that no one is allowed to scale, even with good intentions. Not until we are ready.

We Don't All Have to Go Back

Some of our experience is too sensitive to be dealt with now—or at all—so our repression is in favor of our health. What we call resistance or denial might be in our best interest. We may recall in chemistry class that the sturdiness of the container had to be proportionate to the tension in the chemicals being heated. It is no shame to be too fine a glass to withstand the burning issues of one's past.

For some of us, things may have happened in childhood that are best left unknown. Memories undiscovered may be less harmful than memories confronted when we are too fragile to handle them. To look directly, consciously, at what happened to us might be so terrifying or shocking that we would fall apart, break down, become dysfunctional, or fragment bone by bone, as Emily Dickinson so chillingly describes:

> *There is a pain—so utter—*
> *It swallows substance up—*
> *Then covers the Abyss with Trance—*
> *So Memory can step*
> *Around—across—upon it—*
> *As one within a Swoon—*
> *Goes safely—where an open eye—*
> *Would drop Him—Bone by Bone.*

Our looking away may be our body's self-protective device, a stimulus barrier against what might prove to be too much for us to handle. The fear and danger of knowing who we are, who others are, or what we feel may be reading out internally as confusion. We may not really be confused but simply still not equipped—or ready—to know. Our inner censor is like a guardian angel, protecting us from knowing too much. It is important for us to calibrate the load-bearing capacity of our psyche. How much of ourselves can we safely know?

When nature equipped us humans to grieve losses, she may have thought our greatest loss would be that of our child being killed by a saber-toothed tiger. She may not have foreseen serial killings, terrorism, and holocausts. Our mourning capacity may not yet have evolved enough to process the horrors we are faced with today. Likewise, personally, some of the abuses or losses of our childhood may be larger than our psyche can carry. Some of our griefs might thus be inexhaustible, like those described by Hamlet: "He would drown the stage with tears."

This may be why we are often afraid to know our real feelings or motivations. We may refuse to acknowledge what we cannot handle, as in the biblical story of the sons of Noah. Upon discovering their father drunk and naked in his tent, they avert their eyes as they cover him up, turning away from the fact of their father's alcoholism both psychologically and literally. We may do that or we may allow a glimpse at best, anything but the fearless and sustained gaze that is so challenging in opening to our own truth.

Sometimes it is our ego that gets in the way, not wanting to admit woundedness. Dante saw souls in hell who had refused to repent, a metaphor for the inflated ego's refusal to acknowledge its inadequacies or to ask forgiveness. Indeed, the ego cannot admit brokenness of any kind. How ironic this is, since only when we acknowledge how we are shattered do we find a path to restoration. This irony summons up the paradoxical archetype of redemption, deeply imprinted in our collective human psyche, whereby healing happens through our wounds. This paradox is a way of seeing that the psyche is oriented toward wholeness, that the universe, where our psyches began, is friendly.

The redemptive possibilities thrive best when we begin by admitting our woundedness, without the need to dredge up memories until they come naturally. It usually takes a long siege before the armor of necessary protection or the edifice of the frightened ego can be dismantled and its stones reused to build a healthy self, one unadorned by the defenses that have become the raw material of our transferences.

We grow in our ability to know ourselves as we stabilize our lives through psychological work and spiritual practices. We can then gradually let in more and more about our past. There is a touching synchronicity in the fact that we know more as we can handle more. That synchronicity is the guardian angel, archetype of the friendly universe, who ever so gently crafts a sacred opening in our wounded heart.

Practice
Honoring Timing and Lifestyle

To be present with ourselves with no attempt to change anything is mindful awareness. Such mindfulness becomes a healing paradox, since it can lead us to a natural shift into transformation. Our loyalty to the here and now opens a safe space, provides a context for future readiness.

How does mindful awareness lead to transformation? Staying with our own reality reveals the deep structures of our mind and our world. We see how they flow from causes and conditions. We realize their interdependence. Recognition of interdependence is recognition of emptiness—that is, everything is empty of independence; all is contingent on all. We notice how our clinging leads to suffering, because it becomes caught in the illusion of a separate independent reality and one that will satisfy us when all is unsatisfactory. Mindfulness is an entire course in Buddhism.

It is a Buddhist practice to engage in "direct looking" and then in resting in what we do not find. In this practice, we sit silently, with attention to our breath, and notice stillness, thoughts, and appearances in turn. We see the whom, what, when, and where we have embroidered around them. We let go of those concerns one by one. We let go of attaching ourselves to our concepts about them. Then we enter the emptiness, the stillness that results. This means seeing a reality just as it is rather than one that is filled in with our mind-sets and projections. It is calm abiding in an emptiness that is spacious and contented.

We see our stories in the same way, as real in the conventional sense but as ultimately empty of—free of—concepts. This cutting through is how we open a space by which sanity and wisdom can come through. In that no-place-in-particular, we finally, fully rest.

Practice
Identifying What Is Missing

A second practice has to do with the sense of something missing in our lifestyle or in our relationships. This can take any of four forms:

1. *We know that something is missing and we know what it is.* Here our work is to keep our eye out for fulfillment by placing ourselves in the contexts in which it can happen. We cannot force it; only be open to it.
2. *We know that something is missing and we do not know what it is.* Here our work is to search the ten most commonly required

areas of life to notice which one is lacking and then to work on finding fulfillment of it:

- Do I have a relationship that nurtures me?
- Is my sex life satisfactory?
- Am I in a job that is fulfilling?
- Am I in a living situation that is comfortable?
- Do I have a healthy lifestyle with no addictions?
- Do I have satisfactory connections with family and friends including physical holding?
- Do I have hobbies or engage in activities, for example sports, that enliven me?
- Am I living life with integrity, honesty, and a good conscience?
- Am I making a contribution to the world by being of service to others?
- Have I found a spirituality or religion that feeds my soul?

3. *We did not know that anything was missing but something has come along that nurtures us and we now realize what had been missing.*

    Our practice here is simply gratitude.

4. *We do not feel that anything is missing.*

    Our practice is gratitude for how good life feels so far while still maintaining mindful attentiveness to what may be revealed next.

> *At daybreak, gazing at the moon,*
> *So alone in the sky,*
> *I finally knew myself all the way,*
> *Nothing now left out.*
> —Izumi Shikibu (tenth century)

8

The Physical Dimension

The truth about our childhood is stored up in our body and though we can repress it, we can never alter it. Our intellect can be deceived, our feelings manipulated, our perception confused, our body tricked with medication. But someday the body will present its bill for it remains as incorruptible as the child who accepts no compromises or excuses, and it will not stop tormenting us until we stop evading the truth.

—Alice Miller

Jung uses the phrase "somatic unconscious" to refer to the transference reactions that manifest as physical sensations in the body, which is the most visible form of our unconscious life. The primitive dimension of transference reveals itself in our organic reactions: "I feel her words hitting me in the pit of my stomach." "I tremble when I hear his voice." We feel a tightness in our breath or in our neck as someone comes at us in anger. We feel a weakening of the knees as we see someone on whom we have a crush or with whom we were recently in a relationship that ended badly. During a massage we suddenly burst into tears. We feel a thrill of excitement as we listen to a sweet-talking lover who promises us the moon.

These physical reactions may be a signal that transference is occurring, that there is more going on than can be accounted for by present events or the people enacting them. The body reacts to excitement or trauma no matter how the mind may minimize or rationalize things. We experience cellular reactions that have been stored in us since infancy, all representing unprocessed or unfinished events and feelings. They arise and greet us in the present, bill in hand, and ask for full or partial payment. In a sense, our bodies are like credit cards to which we've been charging items for a lifetime. Eventually, present-day experiences present us with our invoice. Our bodies recall what our minds have forgotten, and physical reactions help us locate our psychological work or explore our past with more care and attention. As Freud said, "The body never lies." Our first sense of self is bodily. Indeed, Freud saw the ego as primarily a "body ego."

How does this body-ego help us? Catharsis, a release of pent-up emotions, is a bodily event, not simply a verbal or mental one. Talk therapy or other helping techniques work best when they become vehicles that carry us into the somatic level of experience. Then addressing, processing, resolving, and integrating is about a more fully conscious, more bodily aware feeling that is opened. The ego is less likely to be on the defensive when it feels it is in a safe container, a holding environment such as therapy, an intimate relationship, or a spiritual community.

Our visceral reaction tells us our truth. Our mind reports only the stock phrases. For instance, our mind says, "It's no big deal." But when we check in with our bodily reaction, we detect anger (perhaps in the form of a clenched jaw or a tightened fist). That hitting upon the truth opens our energy to feel our anger consciously, and we may declare, "I am enraged at them." To disregard that feeling may lead to a depression, while our mental attitude is characterized by confusion. It is interesting to note that in some Southeast Asian countries, depression is believed to be produced by ancestors who were not mourned sufficiently. This is certainly a metaphor for the unfinished emotional business that lurks behind some of our mysterious moods.

The influence of our past is not purely mental. Our body has permanently recorded a bodily sense of who Mom and Dad were to us. We know deep down whether they ever really "got" us or not. The reason we store such information is that attunement with our original caregivers was crucial to our development. We also hold the information because we hope that someday what was missing will be given to us or what was given will be repeated. Some of us are lost in a despair about finding attunement in relationships now, but that does not cancel or expunge our unconscious recollection. This happens because the way our parents treated us became part of our enduring belief about what to expect from others and the world.

My history is not simply a mental memory of what I learned or of what happened to me. It is a fleshly record. So the working through of the transference includes a somatic dimension. The work is to get past our past physically. Here is an example: Our controlling mother certainly also protected us. The price of her protection was our silence in the face of her infringements on our boundaries. Now when we contemplate confronting an authority figure at work, it is equivalent to chancing a major abandonment or loss. In fact, we might have seismic reactions in our body at the very idea of speaking up to our own mother even now. The body is not as easily convinced of safety as the mind. We are challenged in working through our transferences to let the work reach into us somatically. How is this done?

A somatic consciousness means attention to how we live as embodied beings. We find out so much about ourselves from the way we move, walk, breathe, and carry ourselves. Our stresses both from childhood and in the present are encoded in our bodies. They read out as muscle tension, as inhibited bodily movements, as constrictions in our posture and breathing. How we are embodied gives us crucial information about our unconscious processes. We can pay attention to our bodily messages by noticing and noting them. This is how we follow Jung's recommendation that we "give the body its due."

All we really need is a context of safety shown by the five A's as we listen to what our body wants to tell us. We can learn to notice the bodily resonance to our past experience and how it impacts the present. It certainly helps to have a therapist or friend with a keen sense of somatic resonance to what we are feeling. Then, by accompaniment, touch, and encouragement we move more easily into body-mind health.

Somatic therapy is useful in our work on ourselves in that it focuses on how the body acts and looks. It inquires into what the body is communicating. A mindful awareness of stresses and of our structural patterns can lead to letting go of our physical inhibitions. We might then feel more spacious within, less afraid to look like who we are, even when our body image does not match the Hollywood version of beauty or youth. As we let go of our tense binding places and relax into a comfortableness with ourselves, transferences may begin to surface. We contact them through the march into our consciousness of memories and feelings that are tied to events and persons from our past. As we allow the parade of feelings to pass through us and to twirl their batons in us, we stride more exuberantly.

> *Your physically felt body is in fact part of a gigantic system of here and other places, now and other times, you and other people—in fact, the whole universe. This sense of being bodily alive in a vast system is the body as it is felt from the inside.*
> —Eugene Gendlin

How the Brain Figures In

The Brain has Corridors—surpassing
Material Place—
> —Emily Dickinson

Recent scientific research has allowed us to understand the physiological dimension of transference in the brain. Emotional reactions are stored as memories in the amygdala, a structure in the limbic system of the brain that becomes functional perhaps as early as birth. Experiences of the past therefore remain physically present in our body, mind, and behavior as part of the landscape of our personality. A landscape becomes what it is because of years of weather. Our psyches operate in the same way. We are the way we are because of all the conditions we have weathered. We are permanently affected by the events, traumas, and memories of childhood. We store a thick album of old photos inside our bodies, not just in the trunk in the attic.

The human personality is thus not a solid reality but a pattern that keeps changing in accord with time and circumstance. It is not like a statue, done once and for all, but more like a melody-line, done but also continually changing in timbre and rendition. We are stably one as the Moonlight Sonata is one. Yet we are each individual versions and we are not the same from one day to the next. The Moonlight Sonata played by Glenn Gould varies in style from that played by Claudio Abbado. In addition, how each artist performed while recording the Beethoven piece on Monday differs from how it will sound on Saturday night at the concert.

What about stress and fear? They release cortisol, a hormone secreted by the adrenal glands. A state of high alert also releases the neurotransmitter norepinephrine, a chemical that carries electrical impulses across our brain synapses. These mental reactions prepare us to face what we perceive as danger, whether or not it is real. They do this by bringing us fully into the present and fine-tuning our reactions so that we can more readily fight or flee.

Events in the past that were threatening, abusive, or overwhelming produce lifelong somatic effects such as anxiety, depression, a need for constant vigilance, and so on. Processing in the neocortex, where words and logic reside, does not reach the midbrain, where these inner reactions are occurring or recurring. So we cannot talk ourselves out of cellularly recorded information. In fact, during stress there is a decrease in oxygen to the left hemisphere of the brain, and an increase in the right hemisphere, where our emotions and bodily reactions occur. This may explain why, now as adults, we are tongue-tied in states of high arousal, both by fear and desire. We become immobilized instead of fighting or fleeing. We lose the option of standing up for ourselves or even of running for safety. We are as paralyzed as we were when we heard our drunken dad stumble into the house and we wondered what he would do to us this time.

The hippocampus integrates implicit memories into a comprehensible whole. When it is blocked by trauma or high stress, an event cannot be fully processed. *These are all indicators of the vulnerability of memory to factors that are beyond our control.* For instance, a depressed person in a relationship may forget or lose interest in plans the couple have made together. This is not a sign of being confused or capricious. Part of clinical depression is to lose the ability to recall plans or sustain enthusiasms.

The hippocampus is located in the midbrain. There memories of our personal history are put into a correct space-time sequence: what, where, how, when things happened. This is where short-term memory is stored in a correctly short-term way. When long-term high stress is suffered in childhood, there is cell loss to the hippocampus. This means that *something that is past is revived in us now as if it were a short-term memory, giving us the impression that something is happening now that actually happened long ago, the very definition of transference.*

That sense of *present* danger increases our stress. In addition, norepinephrine helps us keenly recall dangerous events and our fear reactions in our long-term memory so we can use what we learned before as we face danger in the immediate present. When recall is sharp, it thus will also seem to us that the past is happening in the present, making a transference seem real.

According to Dr. Allan N. Schore, of the UCLA Medical School, "The human cerebral cortex adds about 70% of its final DNA content after birth, and this expanding brain is directly influenced by early environmental enrichment and social experiences."

Who we are is not simply genetic but is tied to the quality of the early care we received. The prefrontal cortex of the brain, so important for retention of autobiographical memory, is not fully formed until age two. Nonetheless, it goes on developing throughout life. Thus, our biology is optimistic; it confirms that ongoing growth is possible. The prefrontal cortex is responsive to and develops in accord with our interpersonal experiences. This makes it possible to understand why relationships make such an impression on us.

The latest research shows that the qualities that define "self" in us are not located in a single place in our brain, but distributed throughout it. There is no one "thinker" in the control tower, no one operator at a central switchboard. Thus we can practice freedom from the illusion of a solid ego by being open to the boundaryless nature of "me" even in physical terms. A big ego then comes to mean that we include the universe and all that happens in it!

As all that happens to us is met with mindful equanimity, we are less likely to feel caught in the compulsion to avoid some things like the plague and attach to other things for dear life. Now we understand why so many Buddhist masters recommend freedom from preferences. We see this in how Hamlet referred to his friend Horatio as "a man that fortune's buffets and rewards / Hast taken with equal thanks."

Researchers continue to explore how our emotions and memories are stored throughout our bodies and not only in our brain. We are truly body-mind beings, as Shakespeare, too, seems to have guessed (in *Love's Labour's Lost*):

But love . . .
Lives not alone immured in the brain;
But, with the motion of all elements,
Courses as swift as thought in every power,
And gives to every power a double power,
Above their functions and their offices.

Practice
Alternatives to Freezing Up

When we are stuck in hyperarousal, our coping defenses—to fight or flee—cannot be mobilized, so we freeze. A chronic state of being prepared for danger means that our reaction to danger cannot move to the next phase, that of dealing with it. Trauma interrupts that natural progression from arousal to reaction/defense. *When we are constantly on guard, we are trapped in the freeze response, which explains why some people do not move on or take action against abuse in adult relationships.* We call them victims but they may have very little choice, so they really deserve our compassion. And that applies to ourselves too if we are caught that way.

We are not alone, nor is this new to us humans, as even the Declaration of Independence shows: " . . . all experience has shown, that mankind are more disposed to suffer, while evils are sufferable, than to right themselves by abolishing the forms to which they are accustomed." *Our brain makes it seem that this stressful event is one and the same as the original event it resembles, and that we are living it not as adults in this decade but as powerless children from olden days.* Our life is sometimes more resemblance than reality. What compassion we deserve, and fail to give ourselves, for our predicament as stressed humans whose brains, intending to aid us, can so misrepresent our truth.

We can find an alternative to freezing and becoming powerless in the face of fear. It is to stay, to stay put, to stand our ground. This means staying with the truth of our experience. In the film *The Last Kiss,* we see the metaphor of staying very clearly. A young couple face a crisis. The man has been unfaithful and the woman has kicked him out of the house. He knows the relationship is valuable and that they do love each other. He wants to work things out and he wants forgiveness, so he sits on the porch, telling his partner he will not leave until she is ready to talk it all out with him. His remaining on that porch, rain or shine, night and day, lets her know he is seriously repentant. After a suitable interval, she lets him in. I see this as a powerful metaphor of staying and its effect. We stay put, often in silence, and a door opens.

When a stressful, threatening event occurs, we cannot always access our powers to fight or flee. Instead, we may freeze like a deer in the headlights. We can notice this inclination and be ready for it the next time stress happens. When it does, we can breathe deeply, pause rather than freeze, and within a minute make some kind of move, even if it is simply to move our bodies into a new position—which may be all we are capable of. We can then walk with a focused awareness of each step as we place each foot firmly and rhythmically on the earth. Simply doing this in rhythm with our breathing leads to clarity and resolve. We recall Saint Augustine's phrase: "It is solved by walking." We keep walking till we feel ready to make a choice.

After the walking, we sit mindfully and consider all that has happened. We recall the grip of our stress, and picture ourselves as we walked into it. We affirm that it has lost its power to hold us back from choices.

We can also practice beforehand, at any time, with the image of a compass:

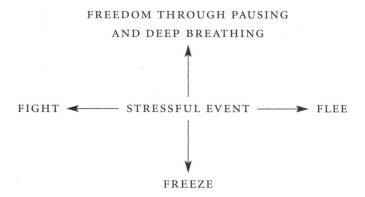

FREEDOM THROUGH PAUSING
AND DEEP BREATHING

FIGHT ◄——— STRESSFUL EVENT ———► FLEE

FREEZE

We see ourselves on the stress compass and imagine ourselves walking around it with ease. We begin in the north quadrant of freedom to choose with perspective and time to pause. This is the neutral corner where we are safe and yet ready to fight. Then we move down to the stressful event matter-of-factly, no longer intimidated by the stressful energy. Then we move south, recalling how we have been frozen at times, doing nothing when choices had to be made. Then we come back up to the center and see ourselves moving *through* stressful events with no *compulsion* to flee or fight. We fully imagine both options and see ourselves as stalwart enough to choose either one if it seems appropriate. Then we come back north and return to being free.

Now we have four choices when we meet up with stress rather than one. We may have a favored style of reacting in times of stress; for instance, we react with a hair trigger for fighting. The choice for freedom from these polar opposites of hasty action, on the one hand, and running because of intimidation, on the other, is the choice not to have to fight or to flee unless we want to. We also do not have to be stymied and to freeze in our tracks; rather we move toward the issue and handle it. Finally, in accord with our commitment to loving-kindness we state an intention and aspiration that all beings everywhere find the same freedom that we have found or are beginning to find. We want the whole world to move along with us.

The practice is enriched when we decide to go north first in every circumstance. We pause in the face of any stimulus so we can get our bearings. Then we are ready to choose whether to fight or flee. We are no longer on automatic pilot, compelled to act in our habitual ways. The pause is our freedom of choice. Then we move into the second part of the practice, to make the choice that has safety and loving-kindness for ourselves and others. For instance, suppose that, up to now, every time someone has cut us off in traffic, we have become enraged and chased him down. Now we pause and let our adrenaline subside a little. Then we notice it is easy to let him pass and wish him the best. The north star has not only steadied us but granted us its equanimity.

The only thing we have to fear is fear itself—nameless, unreasoning, unjustified terror which paralyzes needed efforts to convert retreat into advance.
    —Franklin Delano Roosevelt, First Inaugural Address, 1933

9

Our Yearning for Both Comfort and Challenge

Learn, little boy, to know your mother by her smile.
—Virgil, *Fourth Eclogue*

We need the cheers and sense of belonging from our teammates before we can step up to the plate with confidence and do our best. We need the security of standing at home base before we can face what life may pitch in our direction. In order to grow up, we require a holding environment in which we feel we are loved and protected for all the time it takes to find out who we are. These are the *comforts* that help us trust others. We also need a nudge from the nest so we can go out into the world and open to the full expanse of who we can be. This is the *challenge* that makes it possible for us to trust ourselves. We notice that we are ready and willing to accept the challenge to fly *because* we were in a nest, a holding environment wherein we felt safe.

Throughout life, in relationships, jobs, hobbies, religion, and in almost any enterprise, we continue to benefit from these same two important components of personal change. We need the comfort of safety and the challenge of risk. With comfort only, we do not stretch to our full magnitude. With challenge only, we do not relax into full ease or equilibrium.

We were held in the womb. Our birth was felt as an expulsion. Suddenly the bottom fell out of our comfortable world and we were forced to make our first trip downward. Our birth process was an end as well as a beginning, a loss as well as a gain. We entered the world as mourners but also as pioneers. Indeed, our loss of the comfortable womb became the exciting reward of entry into a larger and more luminous world. The same mother who held us in her womb held us in her arms and we saw her smile. The journey was worth it. The paradox of journey remains throughout life: we have to face the challenge of giving up an outmoded comfort for a new comfort to be followed by a new challenge.

An infant who is greeted at birth with the Leboyer technique of being held tenderly in warm water will feel a sense of continuity with the watery intrauterine world from which he just emerged. This may register in the cells of his body as a serene assurance that change is not so dangerous, since restoration is always possible. The baby—*you and I?*—who was immediately slapped, dosed with silver nitrate, cleaned, placed on a cold scale, dressed, wrapped, and braceleted may feel the new world as quite unfriendly. Shakespeare described the infant's plight when he said that we cry when we are born because we are come aboard "this ship of fools." This baby does not have the same sense of how restoration is possible. His cells may be registering a jolt, not a journey; a sterile routine, not a warm welcome.

Our physical birth may happen in a few hours, but our psychological birth is a lifetime operation. It happens in three stages reflecting those of the heroic journey: separation, individuation, and reunion. We emerge from fusion/symbiosis in the womb and in infancy into gradual independence as toddlers and then into interdependence in adolescence and adulthood.

Thus, the journey toward human maturation is a series both of losses of comfort and presentations of challenges. The ironic dilemma of our predicament is touching: A sense of separateness is necessary for growth, yet we are never totally free of our longing for the comfort of what parents give. At the same time, an inner sense of our separate identity leads us to step out on our own while maintaining our connection with others.

Comfort in childhood was associated with a holding environment in which we felt secure, were not at the mercy of abusers, noticed that our needs were welcomed and fulfilled, were allowed personal options rather than being constantly controlled, felt our authentic self to be the object of our parents' love and curiosity rather than something to be molded into what they believed to be the right personality for us to portray. Our parents mirrored us with mindfulness rather than censured or manipulated us with mind games.

The object-relations theorist Margaret Mahler calls the holding behavior of mother "the midwife of individuation, of psychological birth." Freud used a pleasing barnyard analogy when he noted that the unhatched chick has all it requires within its shell yet it still needs the mother hen's warmth to facilitate and complete its emergence into the world. The comfort of the warm breast makes possible the chick's gingerly steps onto the rugged earth. It is no different for us.

The developmental task of separation is healthy disengagement from symbiosis, fusion, and being held in the arms of mother. It becomes an enduring sense of personal differentiation and demarcation in regard to the external world. This is where we learn to maintain boundaries around ourselves while still relating to others.

Sometimes mothers give us the comfort and fathers give us the push. Fathers often play the role of the one who brings us out into the world, as was shown in the movie *Bambi*. Sometimes it is reversed and mothers fulfill this for us. Sometimes we find only comfort and security or only the challenge of being on our own. Our original experience of comfort and challenge weighs in heavily when it comes to how we will design our adult relationships, our career choices, our religious orientation, our place in social groups, indeed how we decide almost everything.

We look for relationships that both comfort and challenge us, as happened in our childhood or in a recent relationship experience. If we received a good-enough experience of holding and nudging, one that was fairly reasonably proportioned in early life, we will possess the knack of knowing where and how to combine them in our present life situation. Healthy people are always seeking to be both held and dared. They are not embarrassed that they still need embraces and not afraid of the risks in venturing out alone.

The fulfillment of the comfort need makes it feel safe to be ourselves: "The world offers what I need." The fulfillment of the challenge need allows us to feel confidence in ourselves: "I have resources within." The fulfillment of both make for serenity and self-esteem. We are serene in the comfort of having what we need. We grow in self-esteem as we notice we are willing and able to face challenges. Even if we do not always succeed in a venture, we like ourselves for trying.

From time immemorial, people have thrived by combining comfort and challenge. Early people spent the day hunting and working. At night they sat around the fire telling stories and sharing the safety and joy of community. It is important to each of us to find ways to include comfort/relaxation in the tasks that challenge us. Each day works best for us when it includes that same combination. The challenges stretch us and the comforts unwind us, which is exactly how a guitar is tuned to make music.

We can learn to pace our life in accord with our alternating needs for comfort and challenge. If we are stressed by too many challenges, we can pull back and look for nurturance or retreat. If we are bored by a life that has become too relaxed, we can challenge ourselves by launching out into something new. As we read ourselves better, we notice and make the choices that honor our inner timing.

Our dependency/comfort needs are for soothing, empathy, reassurance, and tenderness. Once these needs are fulfilled, our challenge/growth needs can be attended to: creativity, transcendence of limits, striking out on our own, competence in the workaday world, adult relationship commitment, contribution to the world, and spiritual maturation. *I am hoping that this book combines the comfort of empathy in my understanding of you with challenges from the practices I present to you.*

We are born with the potential to experience all human feelings. When our parents hold us with the five A's, they endorse and legitimate what we are feeling, not only in childhood but for ever after. A feeling—be it sadness, anger, fear, or joy—has been installed in us successfully when it is greeted with the five A's from our parents. That is how the holding environment works in favor of our healthy development. "I am safe with my feelings and, best of all, I can bear the painful ones. I am learning to soothe myself." The paradox is that the more we are held in our feelings, the more we are able to hold them ourselves. Comfort from others provides the holding moment that leads to and engenders our ability to face challenges. Potential becomes aptitude.

In infancy we split our image of mother. We believe that there is a comforting mother who fulfills us and that she is different from the frustrating mother who fails to attune to our needs. As late toddlers we begin to realize that both qualities exist in the same person. This skill of combining apparently opposing energies serves us well for the rest of our lives. We can believe that someone may be unpleasant today and pleasant tomorrow, that someone can be an alcoholic today and recovering tomorrow, that the human craving for war can become a desire for peace-making. This is because we recognize the given that people contain both sides of every human coin. This is the valuable coin of hope.

Many of us did not have parents who granted us the five A's: attention, acceptance, appreciation, affection, and allowing. When we finally tell our stories directly and cease using others to tell it for us, we face up to the deficiencies of those who loved us long ago. At the same time, we can become compassionate as we realize our parents were not holding out on us. They may not have had as much to give as we required. They didn't know what we know now about child development. They were certainly accountable for how they treated us, but perhaps not fully so. Certainly, their inadequate treatment of us readied our generation to do the research on child development that has led to the self-help movement! So it was a positive synchronicity after all.

Our work now is our own: we grieve what we missed; we let go of the past; we take full responsibility for our life in the present. The difficult feelings that arise in our grief work can be likened to Cerberus, the intimidating, three-headed dog in Greek mythology who guards the underworld/unconscious. He lets us know we are at the threshold of a region whose geography is mostly unknown. We enter uncharted territory and find out who we were and are. We discover our identity, the feat of heroes. Only then are we ready for marriage to the princess who was waiting for us. She was not waiting because she could not be a heroine and save herself. She was waiting for us to become ourselves so that real she-and-I intimacy could happen.

We find rest in those we love, and we provide a resting place in ourselves for those who love us.
—Saint Bernard of Clairvaux

Practice
How to Grieve and Let Go

Grief work involves the same four steps we have mentioned above regarding working through any psychological issue: we address, process, resolve, and integrate. We *address* by noticing and naming what grieves us. We *process* by expressing our feelings. We *resolve* by letting go. We *integrate* by moving on into relationships that are not so projection or transference laden.

Grief is irreversible. We cannot cancel or change it, yet we try. This is not unhealthy, since we are actually thereby respecting our own capacity for grief. We have to let it come through in its own way and time. This may mean that we avoid it for a while, let it in little by little, or even attempt to deny it. We have to be kind to ourselves in our grief, letting it take the lead, not forcing ourselves into a program meant to release it as soon as possible.

In this practice we look at our feelings and then at the inner shifts that help us let go and go on. As you read through the following reflections on grief and grief work, see what connections you can make with your own life. If a particular paragraph resonates with you, stop to journal your reactions and reflections.

Grief is composed of three feelings:

1. Sadness that something was lost
2. Anger that it was taken away
3. Fear that it will never be replaced

These three feelings can be experienced simultaneously or in any order. Grieving about our unfulfilled needs in childhood means expressing the same three feelings: Sadness that our needs were neglected or unfulfilled, anger at those who did not fulfill them, fear that we might never find a partner who can fulfill us.

The three feelings that comprise grief are like technologies built into us so we can deal with the implacable truths of impermanence, loss, betrayal, and suffering: We have the capacity to be sad because of the given of losses, changes, and endings; we have the capacity to be angry because of the given of betrayal and injustice; we have the capacity to be afraid because it is a given that threat and danger sometimes beset us.

Grief work grants us access to our deepest feelings and to our healthy vulnerability, something so necessary in intimacy. Vulnerability is healthy when it is combined with stability. We feel weak, but our powerlessness does not throw us off course. We are vulnerable, but not as victims.

We are glad rather than ashamed that we are susceptible to human pain without seeking more of it. We open the door to the pangs of love and longing, but we are not doormats. Our hearts are open, but not ripped apart. Our brow is "bloody but unbowed," as the poet William Ernest Henley wrote.

Healthy vulnerability is shown in the same three ways as grief:

1. I am sad that I was hurt.
2. I am angry that I was insulted.
3. I am afraid that I will not be able to get over it.

Such fear is understandable since, as we saw above, there is a feature of grief that is inconsolable: "This is what the Lord says: 'Your wound is incurable, your injury beyond healing'" (Jer. 30:12).

Vulnerability is unhealthy when we restrict the natural flow of our feelings: When we show only sadness, we may feel we are victims. When we show only anger, we are on the defensive and not comfortable with the vulnerability that can make us more lovable. When we show only fear, we seem to be expecting only more mistreatment and we run from relating. The challenge is to experience all three feelings of grief without blame, grudge, or grievance. The three healthy feelings in grief help us in the following ways:

Sadness that is free of blame can help us contact our tender vulnerability as something to be appreciated, as a positive sign of our capacity for love and openness. The negative unhealthy vulnerability brings the sense of being victimized.

Anger becomes useful when it prompts us to become strong enough to break through our fear or when it helps us gain distance from an abuser. It counterbalances the sadness so that we can speak up to abuse or hurt.

Fear can be used positively as a warning signal of danger rather than as an inhibiting or compelling force. Notice that the fear that what we missed will never be replaced also gives us a clue: We may have entered a relationship with the *expectation* that a partner will provide proper and full replacement of what we long for or lost, even though he is not aware of what that may be.

As we express our feelings and let go, we gradually forgive ourselves and others and can get on with life. This happens because our opening to grief, paradoxically, leads to self-comforting. That stabilizes us and we can finally say yes to a world that is bound to deal us gains and losses. We can say to ourselves, "Living through the challenges of life in relationship, I learn to self-soothe. Now my regrets about losses or failures become the building blocks of my sense of personal completeness."

This completeness/wholeness results from the automatic shifts that follow our release of feelings. We notice that we can let go of the charge surrounding what we grieved. Secondly, we let go of blame, grudge, grievance, and the need for revenge—that is, we forgive. Grief and compassion are not meant to be simultaneous but sequential. We cannot easily forgive while we are angry. But once we work through our grief, forgiveness and compassion follow as graces.

Then we notice we can get on with our lives and be more personally grounded, no longer so much at the mercy of transferences that gather around unmet needs, regrets, disappointments, and the grief they carry in their wake. Now we are more able to take care of ourselves and more open to and ready for healthy relationships.

To get on with life also means that our originally devastating issue settles into a straightforward fact. "I am crushed by the realization that my mother didn't love me enough" becomes a yes to that fact as a given of our life, not a shocking insult that can permanently victimize us. Our yes is our liberation into saying, "How can I now love myself enough?" Indeed, every psychological work done, like everything that has happened to us, lands eventually in fact. This does not mean we do not still have feelings, only that they no longer impinge upon us. We shed occasional tears but no longer a flood. Our history has become bearable, the goal of psychological health. When compassion for the depleted or ungiving mom also arises, we have attained a spiritual victory.

A note on anger may help. The dictionary definition of *anger* is "displeasure at injustice." We are actually feeling anger whenever we are unhappy or irritated by what we consider unfair. We may not be able to admit feeling anger, but we usually can admit we don't like something that is happening. We can practice saying aloud to those involved, "I don't like that." That is anger since it is showing displeasure at what we consider to be wrong. It is a simple way to begin, and gradually we will admit we feel anger and become free to show it appropriately and without escalation, even if we still need to do so with a red face, a raised voice, and colorful gestures too.

Grief in the Family

Our ability to grieve depends upon our first experiences of it: What were our original family's reactions to or participation in our grief? In childhood, losses within the family required mutually visible grief. For instance, if when we were still a child, a brother of ours died, it is not enough to grieve this by ourselves. Grief in that instance has to be a family affair. This may be why funerals are public events. We work through our own grief by mirroring one another's grief. We make room for each family member's unique way of showing it. Our parents attend to our grief with affectionate acceptance, appreciation of its weight, and full allowing of us to display it in the way that fits for us. Grief is worked through as they talk openly and often about the lost brother and inquire into our feelings about him rather than wait for us to bring it up. Our parents keep reminding us of his good qualities and how we all miss them. Shakespeare comments on this in *All's Well That Ends Well*:

> *Praising what is lost*
> *Makes the remembrance dear.*

In healthy grief within a family, our parents also check in with us throughout the years about how we were holding the fact of the loss, and they tell us how they hold it. This is what makes a home with a loss into a holding environment of healing. Big gaping holes such as the death of a young family member in childhood are never fully closed, but when they happen in a context of caring love, they become bearable. Resolution then includes surrendering to the given of inconsolability in major grief. This is an example of how the work can be done without the full sewing up of all the loose ends, a project so attractive to the controlling and compulsive ego.

Any feeling reaction of great magnitude may be a condensed set of experiences that bunched over the years into one theme. For example, a series of abandonments in life that have never been fully grieved and let go of will wait for their chance to piggyback onto the most recent version of abandonment. For example, suppose I have a surprisingly strong reaction to the loss of a relationship that seemed relatively unimportant at the time and that certainly did not satisfy me. What I may not realize is that the partner who just left me was more than just herself; she was carrying a meaning similar to that of former, more important partners or of my continually abandoning mother. The griefs cluster now around the loss of her and demand attention. What reads out as a feeling of grief in the present actually refers to the past, the essence of transference.

Physical events can be in this same category. For example, someone may feel fear about undergoing an MRI. All her experiences of suffocation assail her in this moment. Perhaps she almost drowned once, or her uncle often squeezed her with engulfing, though well-meant, affection. An unacknowledged or unresolved event from the past presents its "bill" during an occurrence that resembles it. We are at our best when we are ready to pay the bill either in full or in installments that are in keeping with our own emotional timing.

Of course, in positive transference there are also wonderful bouquets thrown to us. For example, it may be that going on a hike with a best friend feels gloriously enlivening. It is reminiscent of all the many times in nature when we found so much solace and contentment. All the joys of our life so far are budded in us and await their chance to bloom when similar circumstances come along. Perhaps it was wisdom itself that implanted in us a need to repeat.

The hopes and fears of all the years are met in thee tonight.
—Phillips Brooks

Regrets and Disappointments

Transference attempts to make up for past disappointments—and sometimes winds up repeating them. We may have been betrayed or disillusioned by our early caregivers or by a past partner. We look for those who will not disappoint us now. Yet it is a given that people do not always come through. We may regret placing our trust in those who hurt us. We may regret mistakes in life and in relationships and be disappointed in ourselves.

Both regret and disappointment are forms of grief. We can learn to greet them with an unconditional yes. Then our acceptance leads to handling them so that they do not impinge too long upon our happiness.

Regret is repeated grief. Regrets become helpful when we cease trying to rid ourselves of them. Instead, we make a place for them in the context of the five A's. We notice them, accept them, appreciate what they mean, still love ourselves as we are, and allow ourselves to go on with life without being held back by them.

In regret, as in guilt, we feel bad about feeling bad. When regret comes to mind as we recall our past mistakes and poor judgments, we can acknowledge them as passports to humility, ego deflation, and useful learning. When they are experienced in the context of acceptance of the given that we all err, they are not so hard to take. We can say yes to them and thereby to our ever-falling, ever-rising selves. If we and the world had been meant to be perfect, our central human archetype would not be the heroic journey and our world would not be based on evolution!

The third-century Christian theologian Origen proposed the beautiful concept of apocatastasis, that all beings will be converted and saved at the end of time, even the damned, even the demons. For him, hell is not eternal; only divine love is. So all that happens can be redeemed, ultimately used for our good. This can be a metaphor for all the things we have done that we are ashamed of and now regret. They can all be "saved," that is, included in our positive image of ourselves as errant beings who keep finding ways to get back on track.

We can also recall the legends surrounding the Buddhist saint Padmasambhava (whose name means "the lotus-born"), who brought Buddhism to Tibet in the eighth century. Upon his arrival he met up with aggressiveness both in the people and in the demons around them. He did not destroy the demons but instead converted them so they could become protectors. Using a metaphor, we can say that he found lotuses in the muddy depths, a spiritual challenge for all of us. Saint Boniface brought Christianity to Germany, where he found the people worshipping an oak tree. He cut it down but built a chapel from its wood. Saint George killed the menacing dragon and then fed the frightened villagers with its meat to give them its strength. In spiritual maturity we do not destroy, only dismantle and rebuild using the original materials. We redirect energy rather than defeat it.

We all experience disappointments. We most easily develop into healthy people when our disappointments, like all our challenges, happen in a comforting holding environment rather than in isolation. With such accompaniment by those around us, we learn to hold ourselves, to let ourselves be held, and to hold others too. As Shakespeare says in *Henry VI, Part Three:*

> *My pity hath been balm to heal their wounds,*
> *My mildness hath allayed their swelling griefs . . . .*

In childhood, caring parents noticed our disappointments with them and with the world and they helped us name them. They held us in a warm embrace as we wept. They did not criticize us for what we felt, but listened to us and accepted our experience. They appreciated and valued us enough to love us just as we were. We seek relationships now that offer all that. We no longer need a mother when we are adults, but we always need motherly moments and fatherly moments too. What are such moments? They are the times when we are held with the five A's. Those are also the very moments in which we learn to give the five A's to others. The result is intimacy, with all its comfort and challenge.

Practice
Handling Regret and Disappointment

A helpful way to handle regrets is to place them in a larger space than memory provides. Instead of thinking of regrets as happening in our memory, which has narrowed to receive them, we imagine that they have *opened a space for practice.* Then memory is not simply happening to us but is a launching pad for awakening.

Verbally or in our journal, we can say yes to all that has happened to us and to all the choices we made. We can bless and release them without the self-blaming mind-sets of ego. This happens as we settle into equanimity with the reality of what is and what was. Such acceptance of our own reality leads us to take the next step in our lives. Then we know that regret has been integrated.

We have all heard of learning from our mistakes. For instance, we learn not to touch a hot stove. That is a simple lesson based on the reaction of pain. Yet we may keep going back to painful relationships because we have not yet grasped a way to place an original painful relationship in a context of life learning. Instead, we may seek future relationships that are just as bad for us. When this happens, we are in the grasp of a "repetition compulsion," an irresistible need to repeat rather than get beyond our past. How, then, do we learn and change in the area of relationship?

We *address* the problem when we recognize how we seek partners who hurt or disappoint us. We *process* the problem as we grieve for ourselves and realize that our choices hearken back to the past. Within a relationship, *resolving* includes making a new agreement, breaking out of the dysfunctional pattern. We resolve by letting go of the latest candidate to continue the history of hurt, with no retaliation but with compassion for ourselves and her. We *integrate* when we insist that others honor our boundaries and not hurt us purposely. This leads to an increase in self-esteem. Now we see how we grow from our mistakes, not just learn from them.

Some spiritual practices place the emphasis on letting go of attachment so that we will not experience disappointment at all or ever again. This seems suspiciously like an entitlement to an exemption from a given of life. Without disappointment, we might lose opportunities to become people of more depth, character, and compassion. Do we really want to be so careful about avoiding suffering that we become closed to the kinds of pain that humans were meant to feel so they could grow? Do we want a spiritual practice that makes us so far removed from the rest of humanity that we cannot understand their suffering? Do we really want to use our spiritual practice to gain full control over human hurt?

In my own life I have noticed that my worries and regrets have a shorter shelf life now than they did before I began my spiritual practices. The nagging thoughts lose their wallop faster than they used to. The regrets become flatlined memories rather than the obsessive barbs that once they were. This has been a welcome boon, and I give thanks when I

notice it. The attitude of gratitude seems to compel the demons to retreat sooner and to persuade the angels to hang around longer.

Our spiritual practice can mature so much that it now grants us the
graces of healthy comfort in our griefs and healthy challenges on our
journey. This happens as we allow our regrets and disappointments and
grieve them. Then we say with the Nobel laureate Dag Hammarskjöld:

> *For all that has been: Thanks.*
> *For all that shall be: Yes.*

10

Mirrors and Ideals

Two key steps in our early psychological development are being mirrored by others and idealizing others. In this chapter we will see how they become forms of transference.

One of our major focuses in early-life transference is to find someone who can understand and mirror us. This happens when our parents give us the five A's. Later in life, we will, in turn, be able to mirror the adults in our relationships.

Another focus of transference is toward someone we can admire and then imitate. In early childhood we admire our parents' powers and gradually internalize them. The result is that we can nurture ourselves as they nurture us. Later, in relationships, we will be able to nurture others.

By contemplating these two strands of development in our early life—mirroring from others, which leads to trust, and admiration of others, which leads to self-nurturance—we can better understand our transferences now. We still look for those who can mirror us as our parents did or did not. We still look for those we can admire as we admired or did not admire our parents. As we have been seeing, our transferences are based on what we did receive and want more of or what we missed out on and want to make up for.

Our Search for Mirroring Love

Our basic trust flows from an ongoing belief in the capacity of the world to grant us a fulfillment of our needs. This basic trust is gained, or rather inputted into us, early in life through a series of reliable fulfillments of our needs by our parents. Our parents also build our trust in them when they show that they understand us. For instance, they see we are afraid, imitate our look of fear, and say, "It's scary, isn't it? It's OK to feel scared." This is mirroring, or attuning to our feelings. Attunement means that someone has understood us and aligned her feelings to ours. The same parent holds us in our fear and gives us thereby a sense of safety. The mirroring love has led to a loving action. (This will be the style of our compassion all through life. We see pain in others and it reads out on our face too, and we then engage in an action that helps.)

"Object permanence" is a cognitive skill that was identified by the developmental psychologist Jean Piaget in babies of eighteen months. By then, the baby realizes that when the ball rolls behind the sofa, it does not disappear but can be found again intact. This realization then applies in his mind to the reliability of the mother who went to work or simply left the room. Absence does not mean disappearance, only distance, usually temporary.

The emotional equivalent of object permanence is the ability to trust that our bond with the mother we rely on remains intact even when she is away, angry, or out of sight. This is one way of describing what in psychology is called "object constancy," our belief that the object of our love and trust is constant in her connection to us, present even if absent, loving us even if angry. This happens because the bond we have come to need so much *lives on in us.* We have internalized the mirroring love of our parent and the comfort it gives. Our security in now based on an *inner* experience.

In adult life, when someone shows trustworthiness, we receive it and feel appreciation. If we notice that someone is untrustworthy and has betrayed us, we withhold our trust. This is the adult style of trust as a basis for relationship: our trust is in *ourselves* rather than only in a partner. Indeed, unconditional trust in a partner is a dangerous disregard of the given of life that people are not always trustworthy or reliable. As we say yes more and more to that given, we reconcile ourselves to *moments* of reliability in relationship for which we are appreciative and moments of unreliability for which we grieve without retaliating.

As we live serenely with the impermanence built into human behavior, we also no longer blame a parent who could not be there for us all the time, nor do we look for a partner who will do so now. The phrase "all the time" is no longer in the vocabulary of an adult in relationship.

Because of our inner sense of security, we can experience occasional personal betrayal and deceit, even while our ongoing trust in humankind endures, not affected by what any specific individual may do. In this sense, basic trust is an empowering resource. While certain partners may hurt us, they cannot undo the abiding trust that we continue to carry so steadfastly toward the human world. We become able to hold others with a relaxed grasp, not compulsively or coercively as if we needed to hold on for dear life. Buddhist writer Stephen T. Butterfield wrote, "Since no relationship can be made entirely safe and secure . . . this has to mean trust in one's own ability to use any consequence, including betrayal, as a means for waking up."

If we are unable to handle the given of others being temporarily unavailable to us, we are in a sense handicapped in relationships. Without strong reserves of ongoing trust in ourselves as worthy of trust, we may believe that someone is abandoning us when she may not be doing that at all. Disapproval, too, may be experienced as a form of abandonment. The association of disapproval with abandonment may explain why some of us feel such terror when someone frowns at us, criticizes us, or turns away from us.

> *My true love hath my heart, and I have his,*
> *By just exchange, one for the other given . . . .*
> *His heart in me, keeps me and him in one . . .*
> *He loves my heart for once it was his own:*
> *I cherish his, because in me it bides . . . .*
> —Sir Philip Sidney

Can't Live without You

Without basic trust in ourselves, we may come to believe that we will fall apart when the one person we need so much has disappeared. We imagine that we can only survive with and in her physical company. We have nothing going for us on our own.

We may feel terror or panic when we sense or see that our desperately needed connection has been permanently wrecked. This is because, originally, we required a holding environment to survive, so our whole existence was in jeopardy if the one we needed was lost to us, her arms never again around us, her eyes no longer gazing lovingly and fixedly upon us. Our need for connection helps us understand why it is so hard to let go of others all through life, especially at the ending of a relationship. It is especially hard to let go when we don't quite know what we were holding on to to begin with.

We are terrified not because we are cowards or overly dependent but because we are human and understand how that *necessitates* a life together. This fact may explain why we put up with so much abuse from our family members. We have noticed, in an infallible and enduring way, that no matter what, they are committed to being with us, and such certitude means more to us than any pain they may inflict on us or any criticism they may fire at us. Now we understand this from Zechariah: "If anyone asks, 'What are these wounds on your chest?' the answer will be 'These are the wounds I received in the house of those who loved me'" (Zech. 13:6).

It is a given of relationship that a partner can be sometimes satisfying and sometimes frustrating or disappointing. In unconditional love—love without reserve, love that is not selective—we can remain committed no matter what. Indeed, a partner can still be dearly loved even in times when he cannot fulfill our needs. We can learn mature tolerance of a partner's limits and of her sinister aspects because we learned to trust in the hardiness of the link, no matter how numerous the shortcomings.

The shadow side of trusting an ongoing bond is our tendency to believe there is more there than there really is. This may become codependency when we stay committed to someone who continually abuses us by violence, abandonment, or infidelities. We believe in a connection because of our own neediness, and then we ignore our own boundaries. A second danger in the trust we have built by object constancy is that we may be too quick to believe we should be loyal to someone because, like a parent, he does indeed keep returning to us. This is harmful to us if it means becoming too trusting of our mental version of reality.

Finally, it is object constancy that makes faith possible: We can believe in a divine presence when we feel only absence, believe in the arrival of a comforting grace when we are losing hope. Faith becomes a bridge, the transitional object by which we trust ourselves in the world and feel ever accompanied by a power beyond our ego: "I will fear no evil, for Thou art with me" is how the Twenty-third Psalm expresses it. Even without belief in a personal God, we can have this experience of security by trusting in Buddha mind, in a fellowship of recovery, or in any ineradicable reality behind the appearances of separateness and transitoriness.

A Bridge Appears

By fifteen months, a baby notices the fading of his comforting symbiotic fusion with mother. He sees his separateness and hers. Yet grief is still too complex a feeling to have or tolerate, so he usually expresses his displeasure by restlessness and hyperactivity. Gradually, he learns to cope by continued contact with his parents and by play, especially with toys. We still use relationship, play, and our adult toys for that purpose.

A "transitional object" is a toy or any object that mimics or reminds a child of a loved one who is not always present. A perfect example is the blanket or teddy bear that carries the comfort of mom and home. The toddler carries it everywhere, and thereby, through the power of sensual imagination, always has mom nearby. We will accept substitutes in just that way all our lives.

So many things in adult life may serve this bridging purpose: a car, a pet, a bank account, God, a bottle, a spiritual practice. We may use them now as we did in childhood: to feel secure amid so many uncertainties. In a sense, the phenomenon of transference also acts as a transitional object. By seeing the formerly needed other in the newly needed other, we maintain our connection to the original—a bridge between them—until we can live fully without her.

What follows once we cross the bridge? In object-relations psychology, age eighteen to twenty-four months is characterized by a "rapprochement crisis." This stage happens when we are obliged to give up our narcissistic grandiosity and accept the fact that our parents are not extensions of ourselves nor limbs for the fulfillment of our needs but separate beings who sometimes come through for us and sometimes fail us. Our task is to relate to them from that viewpoint, to form an alliance, a rapprochement.

In the rapprochement crisis we give up the sense of our own and our parents' omnipotence. We feel separation anxiety and yet we are compelled to separate by dictate of our maturing ego. This is certainly a scenario that will happen many times in life. As toddlers we are not able to make it on our own. As adults we are able to walk on or out by ourselves, if we have been doing the work it takes to grow. Then we are not caught in codependent neediness or desperation for connection. We have learned to walk across bridges with or without company.

Where Our Ideals Came From

How do we become individuals who can handle the major life task of taking care of ourselves the way good parents care for their children? We begin that process in early life, between one and a half and three years old, when we idealize and admire our parents for their skill in householding and their competence in caring for us. Gradually, we internalize their skills at caretaking. They model the skills; we incorporate them. Indeed, the idealization of our parents and our internalizing of that idealization leads to generating our own high ideals and moral values. All through life, we idealize others in order to locate our own unopened powers.

All this relates to what in self psychology is called "transmuting internalization." This simply means that we assume/internalize the soothing, nurturing, and confidence-producing qualities of our caregivers. With this skill in place, when we feel threatened, we have something going for us internally that gives us a sense of safety. We do not have to seek only outside for need fulfillment. By internalizing powers, we have the kingdom within us while still benefiting from relationships with others. Internalization is a political act, since it validates the sharing of power.

We make the transition from idealizing to internalizing as our parents show us the five A's repeatedly and consistently. Their joyful love for us is what makes us join them rather than compete with them in achieving competence. We thereby learn to value and trust ourselves without having to compete with those we respect, a valuable quality all through life. As adults, we will not need to look so desperately for security from others. We will not be so demanding in relationships but look for only *some* of our need fulfillment from others, since we are already giving so much to ourselves and finding so much in ourselves. Later, in adult relationships, it will make sense that no more than 25 percent of our need-fulfillment can come from any one person.

We notice that our parents are competent enough to fulfill their own needs when others do not come through for them. Another part of internalizing is learning to fulfill our own needs when our parents fail to do so for us. Unfortunately, some parents are remembered for requiring rather than inspiring. We do not think of them as ideal. Yet at the toddler level of intellect, they might have been quite awesome indeed. Nature, with our best interests in mind, arranged a convenient blindness for us. We did not notice the shadow side of our parents until well after we no longer needed them to help us form our important internalizations. Later, as adults we might not notice our partner's shadow side until after we have produced progeny and met up with our own shady side. All these forms of synchronicity are perhaps other ways evolution uses human timing so beneficially.

The Gift of Self

A coherent sense of self includes the realization of agency and efficacy in the world: "I can persuade others to respond, so I am somebody." This is a way of finding the comfort of personal authentication in a world of others.

Low self-esteem, lack of a stable sense of self, happens as a sense of worthlessness, the belief that we do not have the ability to evoke mirroring from significant others. A lack of original mirroring can make it hard to believe we are lovable, so we doubt our lovability and adequacy all through life. Ever after, we seek others to look up to, never believing in ourselves fully. We repeat our hurt past as we go back to those capable only of unattuned moments, like misdirected piano tuners going back to untunable pianos, not ready to concede that the proper pitch cannot be struck there.

Success in forming basic trust and in internalizing ideals—the topics of the previous two sections—provide us with the very gifts that lead to a stable sense of self. These abilities are also precisely the results of working through our transferences!

- We trust ourselves to receive love and handle disappointment.
- We have self-confidence and ideals to live by and thereby grow in self-respect.
- We are cultivating healthy ambitions that will be our goals in life.
- We are becoming able to put off immediate gratification of our impulses rather than feeling compelled to fulfill them in ways that might harm us.
- We are able to maintain healthy boundaries in our relationships with others.
- We learn to take care of ourselves when others do not come through for us. This is self-soothing, a result of internalizing the soothing powers of our parents toward us.
- We can move on when a partner no longer will come through for us at all.

Paradoxically, the final sign of a coherent sense of self is in the fact that we make room for times when we become destabilized. When we are under stress or in shock, we temporarily lose access to our healthy ego powers and become dysfunctional in some way. This is a normal and common experience for all of us. All that matters is that we have it in us to accept this option as a given and that we recover from it as soon as possible.

Mirroring love from our parents leads to a sense of our own power. We find it in the holding and releasing arms of those who love us. Freud says so touchingly, "Knowing that he is loved by his mother makes the little boy a conquistador." Loving parents later become our keepsakes, appreciated mementos of our past together, still showering us with strength-building affection. We learn to direct to ourselves the same soothing five A's our parents showed us.

Thanks to our basic trust, our internalizing of nurturant powers, the four hurdles we met in chapter 5 can be negotiated: We are secure enough to trust others in their comings and goings. We can give and receive in intimate relationships. We can endure rejection without falling apart and can welcome acceptance without fear. We can let go and move forward in life, since we have so much going for us internally.

When parents mirror a child, her feelings are legitimated. When a child idealizes her parents, her powers are legitimated. Both of these demonstrate the *allowing* part of the five A's of love. We are all participants in how we become ourselves.

How Our Needs Are Transferred

Our need for mirroring, our need for receiving the five A's, and our need for others to look up to become forms of transference. When the need for mirroring is transferred onto others, we run the risk of demanding too much. We might be seeking parental love from someone who can only offer partner love. When idealizing becomes transference, we might look up to someone as a savior. We risk remaining children in our need for someone to believe in. We risk becoming victims if we believe someone will be our refuge and security. When we live in a world of equals, we experience kinship with other humans who, like us, sometimes come through with love, sometimes act admirably, and sometimes do not. This healthy kinship, as we shall see, becomes a third form of transference after mirroring and idealizing.

We transfer onto one another a hope of receiving mirroring based on the success or failure of our parents in providing mirroring love to us. When we feel mirrored by someone on whom we transferred our hope, we experience a *mirroring transference.*

We transfer the idealization of our parents onto others. Inasmuch as healthy internalization of parental powers is a component of establishing a stable sense of self, our idealizing of others is how we keep trying to grow up. This is called an *idealizing transference.* It leads to a *kinship/ twinship transference,* in which we feel a more mature sense of communion and equality with those whom we admired.

These three needs/transferences are examples of how the full opening of ourselves is echo-based, that is, requiring human responsiveness
for full fruition. Like the spherical people in Plato's *Symposium* who were
cut in half by the gods, we are continually seeking a reunion with what is
missing from our potential for wholeness. We hold so many pairs within
us; the psyche is a Noah's ark.

Notice the progression:

Trust, based on being mirrored, leads to our believing that others are
still bonded to us even in their absence. This is our source of comfort
and our path to intimacy.

Idealizing others' competence leads to daring to make it our own.
This is our source of challenge and our path to achieving our ambitions
and goals.

Feeling on a par with others results from mirroring and idealization.
This is the path to self-esteem and a sense of oneness.

Finally, mirroring is related to showing us the five A's and engaging
with us with strong feelings. Each of us wants to be recognized in that
way by both sexes. If this happened only with males in our childhood, we
might now yearn for it from females, or vice versa. Father and uncles engaged with us; mother and sisters did not. This unfulfilled need may later
be transferred. It will appear as a desire to please or be recognized by a female manager at work. It may be transmuted into a sexual fantasy, such
as being dominated—and then held—by an older female. It can become
an argumentativeness or feistiness that induces females to become our
opponents. In each case, we are seeking the emphatic female interest in us
that was missing originally. It may take us many years to notice this and
to identify how we have transferred it onto so many innocent bystanders.

The three most basic forms of transference are all forms of healthy
narcissism in that we are trying to build our own sense of self through
interacting with others. Indeed, all transference is a regression or a renewed attempt to find fulfillment of these same three childhood needs.
We can look at each of the three forms of transference in detail:

MIRRORING transference happens when someone attunes to our
feelings with the five A's. We may respond to receiving the five A's by
transferring onto those who show it to us the hopes we had of find-

ing it in our parents. The loving other is a new parent, this time truly giving and trustworthy. In our valentine we will say, "I always wanted to be loved like this. Thank you."

Attention-seeking may be about finding a way to be mirrored. When we are needy for mirroring of our value or importance, we may talk a lot, feeling the need to tell our story. If others cannot stand this, they might engage in a countertransference reaction of boredom, inattention, or even rejection. They miss their opportunity for showing us the mirroring love we still hope to find. Reliable mirroring is how relationships become unconditional.

IDEALIZING transference happens as we come to admire someone and believe we can share in her power and competence. We transfer onto someone we look up to the same idealizing beliefs we had toward our parents. The signs of idealizing transference at work are praise, appreciation, gifts, compliments: "You are the best partner I have ever had."

This idealizing can take the form of a merger transference, in which we give up our own identity and meld with the other, losing our boundaries in the process. This can happen, for example, when we follow a guru or join a cult. Trustworthy leaders will not take advantage of our human tendency toward idealizing transferences by controlling and brainwashing us devotees. They will redirect our devotion to them to a higher power and to the glory of our own inner potential.

In healthy idealizing transference we project our own powers onto others and then we internalize those powers back into ourselves. When they come back to us, they become our psychic structures, that is, the feelings and attitudes that make us our unique selves, what constitutes our own identity.

TWINSHIP, or alter-ego transference, is a natural progression from the idealizing transference. Twinship is not a new transference, simply an extension and completion of the idealizing process. It refers to the point at which the idealized person is perceived as an equal.

For instance, we looked up to our parents and idealized them in childhood; now we respect them but as co-adults.

Twinship also relates to the mirroring transference since it includes the sense of an enduring connection with our original source of nurturance. It can be considered a third chance for us to develop a coherent sense of self from the rubble of failures in mirroring or idealizing. We find just the person who mirrors our potential, shows us how to awaken it, and allows us to stand with her as an equal.

There is also a spiritual twinship, in which we begin to see the connectedness among all of us humans, a liberation from xenophobia. Even after we work through transference and relate to someone in all her uniqueness, a strong sense of our communion remains. This is what Jung called "the kinship libido," a core instinct for twinship connectedness in our collective psyche.

We engage in mirroring transference to answer the question "Can I trust his strength and be held up by it whether or not I am with him?"

We engage in idealizing transference to answer the question "Can I form an alliance with this powerful being and share in the powers I admire?"

We engage in twinship and answer the question "Am I a peer with both independence and connection?"

To summarize:

Our early needs are:	*They lead to equivalent transferences:*
To have our feelings appreciated: MIRRORING is from our parents to us	We seek MIRRORING transference, in which we find attunement to our feelings from others
To be protected in stress and danger by a power we can respect: IDEALIZATION is from us to our parents	We engage in IDEALIZATION, transference in which we admire and look up to others
To be acknowledged as an equal by those we respect: TWINSHIP is the sign of our coming into our own	We experience TWINSHIP transference, in which we feel we have found a true peer, alter ego, or soul mate.

Transference Meets Us Everywhere

We notice specific qualities in each level of transference:

> Trust that the other can be relied on for the five A's is central in the mirroring transference.
> A wish to be like the other is central in the idealizing transference.
> A belief that we *are* like the other is central in the twinship transference.

The three levels of transference usually follow one another in the same order as happens in our relationship with our parents: In infancy they mirror us. When we are children, we idealize them. When we are adults, our relationship is on an equal footing.

The same three levels in the same order happen in a love relationship, reflecting the stages of the heroic journey: In the romance phase we mirror each other and thereby build trust. Gradually, in romantic love, we also idealize each other, not quite noticing each other's defects nor the possibility of a shadow side. In the struggle phase of a relationship we see each other's shadow quite vividly. We then accept the dark as well as the bright potentials of the other and acknowledge the same qualities in ourselves. Finally, the oneness/twinship becomes a soulful connection and the foundation of authentic intimacy. Twinship is the way you-and-I relationships—those free of transferences and projection—happen.

The three forms of transference also reflect exactly the three needs to be fulfilled if we are to build a stable sense of self: We require mirroring to grow in self-confidence. We have to have someone to look up to, idealize, if we are to establish our own ideals. We find a sense of belonging necessary so that we can feel that we are not outsiders but included, a deeper instance of being connected.

The stages of recovery in Alcoholics Anonymous successfully combine all three forms of transference. Mirroring transference happens when others listen empathically to the new member. Idealizing transference happens when the long-sober members show the work they have put into recovering and the now-sober members admire them for it and may choose them as sponsors. Twinship transference happens when a group of recovering members of the program see one another as equals.

The three levels of transference also appear strongly in religion. For instance, we might feel loved and understood by God, whom we see as a guardian/companion/parent, the equivalent of divine mirroring. In addition, we look up to God as perfect and infinitely compassionate. Then we gradually realize that God is a metaphor for our own inner yearning for and calling to bring loving-kindness into the world around us. We have moved from looking up to heaven for God to looking into our own hearts and into nature and then realizing that the divine presence is one with the depths of who we are and what the universe is.

In Buddhism, we see the same progression. We bow before Buddha's statue and offer flowers and incense. Soon we notice that his enlightened state and the wisdom and compassion that flow from it are in us. Then we act in the world as he did, with mindfulness and loving-kindness. When we acknowledge that, we are Buddha in this day and age, and we have moved along the spiritual path from idealizing to metaphor to action.

The three forms of transference and of building a healthy ego have one thing in common: the need for others. This is an alternative to the harsh and puritanical insistence on individualism or rugged self-reliance. The fact that all through life we still seek the fulfillment of these three needs is not a sign of a defect in us. It shows that we have not despaired. We are still reaching out, no matter how often we have been rebuffed. We are still opening our heart, no matter how often it has been wounded. We are unconditional in our trust that there is a human out there who will be human toward us. That is not foolish fantasy or wishful thinking but wholesome hope.

> *Everything is arbitrary except metaphor, which detects the essential kinship of all things.*
> —Charles Simic

Practice
New Ways of Trusting

Make journal entries about your progress in the following areas of practice:

1. Instead of trusting in someone as infallibly and permanently there for us, we can begin to trust in *moments* of trustworthiness

with a variety of people. We do not stop trusting; that would make us less human, less warmly connected to others. We seek not perfect but closer and closer approximations of togetherness.

2. Mindfulness meditation leads us to locate and appreciate direct experience of the here and now. We let go of our conception of how reality is, should be, or can be. We calmly abide in the way it is right now. We notice that we cannot hold on to how it is, that our presence in reality, like reality itself, is fleeting. We notice our inability to focus on any one thing for very long. This is not a defect in us; this is a commentary on the transitory nature of reality. Our practice of moment-to-moment mindfulness helps us make peace with the temporary, both in how reality displays itself to us and in how we display ourselves to one another.

Practice
Whom Do We Trust?

Another practice is to make a list of the people you trust and the reasons you trust them. Ask yourself if you can handle each of them letting you down in some way. Place an intention of appreciating moments of trustworthiness in each of these relationships. Let yourself feel gratitude for the loyalty they have already shown you. Let yourself be ready for the possibility that they may not always come through for you as you desire them to. Your practice is your reward.

Look at yourself. In what areas are you a trustworthy steward of your own body, mind, and soul? Can you make changes in your lifestyle that make you a more reliable shepherd of yourself?

Consider this question: are my relationships based on my unconditional trust in others? This may be a child's style. Try this: I trust myself to receive loving-kindness when it is shown to me and to handle betrayal when that happens by grieving it and not retaliating because of it.

We can also practice becoming aware of our own countertransference, how we react to others who seek to transfer their needs onto us. When others look for mirroring from us and we cannot give it, when they look up to us and we cannot handle it, when they want to be like us and we cannot stand it, those are countertransference reactions. When others look to us for mirroring or idealize us and we use this to manipulate or control them, that is also a countertransference reaction.

In our response to others' idealization of us, we might show appreciation and/or become a mentor or sponsor as in a Twelve-Step program. These are healthy responses to the idealizing transference of others onto us. It takes courage and humility to accept the praise we deserve and to hold it with integrity. We aspire to these virtues using statements like this: "May I accept and appreciate the love and admiration others show me. May I never take advantage of it. May I show love to others and admiration of others freely and fearlessly. May all beings give and receive love in ways that benefit all of us."

Practice
Examining Our Ideals

This practice is for people who are overly enamored of a leader or guru or even of an intimate partner.

A person whom we honor as a leader morphs easily into the parent, lover, or savior archetype. We transfer onto our guru powers that he may not have. These powers signal the loss of our own powers, with the consequent danger that we may then become slavishly attached.

If the mentor or guru disappoints or betrays us in some way, our attraction becomes aversion. This is because these were actually two ends of a single spectrum. The hazard in our feeling attracted is that we imagine that it stands alone, that we are only attracted. In fact, it is directly hooked to its polar opposite, aversion. So we eventually may hate someone as much as we loved him before. The hate is a sign that we have not discharged our full feeling of anger. Once we have, we find ourselves neither drawn to nor turned away from the other. Our hate turns into indifference or compassion.

We are then at the center of the spectrum, the point from which we can spring to the freedom of recovery of our powers. Mindfulness meditation helps us get there, since it is the practice of noticing feelings and thoughts without being compelled to grasp them or repudiate them. Instead, we are witnesses of all the passing show as scenery flashing before us. We are free to look without being so fascinated that we are disempowered nor so aggressive that we want to attack.

It is also important, when we feel anger toward someone because he has hurt or rejected us, to balance our anger by opening to our sadness and our fears. Then the full spectrum of our grief can be embraced. We emerge from that embrace free of the aggression of hate and the vulnerability to be hoodwinked again.

The more I can relax and open up to the world, trusting it and accepting the responsibility that involves responding to its needs—which is what loving it means—the more I feel a part of it, at one with other people; and consequently, others become more inclined to trust and open up to me.

—David Loy

11

Why I Love You But Don't Really See You

It takes courage to see the world in all its tainted glory and still to love it—and even more courage to see it in the one you love.
—Oscar Wilde

Sex and Our Erotic Transferences

Erotic transference is a term used in therapy. It refers to falling for someone because something appealing in his manner, personality, or looks reminds us of someone who fulfilled, or promised to fulfill, our needs in the past. We are conscious of erotic transference, but its origins in our past are unconscious.

We may fall in love with a woman because she seems to be offering us an opportunity for the fulfillment of something we have been wanting or that we had before and want again. In this sense, erotic transference points us to our true needs, perhaps unnoticed, and to our grief, perhaps unexpressed.

By three years old, boys are able to learn to find reassurance and comfort by holding their penises. Perhaps we continue looking there for comfort, which is not wrong or foolish, only limited. We begin to fall into a lifelong illusion about what vast benefits sex can mean to us, give to us, and do for us. Sex has the power of promising much more than it might deliver. It easily becomes more than it was ever meant to be, and we are swept off our feet by the carnival barker it can become.

Sex is natural and a way of experiencing pleasure and showing love. Yet it can become associated with the aggrandizement of ego, the part of us that believes the definitions and promises of the flimflam salesmen: street mentality, media, advertising. We men may then size up our manhood on the basis of our sexual performance or anatomy—an especial danger in midlife. Women may believe their femininity is based on weight or looks. Both women and men may confuse sex with affection. For some people, sex may be the only form in which closeness can feel safe, since they remain in control during it. We notice we can use sex as a weapon, a tactic, a trick. Using sex in such ways is like expecting an appliance to do more than it was built to do—for example, using a hair dryer as a heater. It will work for a while, but eventually it will break down or become dangerously overheated.

Erotic transference reminds us that when a couple is in bed, their two sets of parents are in the bed with them. Thus, familiar phantoms become our strange bedfellows. Since our needs in childhood, the five A's, are the same as those in intimate relationships, the confusion is understandable. Yet a true you-and-I relationship emerges only when we notice who is in bed with us, who is beside us when we are arguing, or who is possessing us when we are kind or mean.

Freud also guessed that erotic transference in therapy, sexualizing a transference reaction, and the experience of love, both draw from the same primal life experiences. Today, researchers on infant behavior and attachment have discovered a striking similarity between certain behaviors within mother-infant bonding and those of adult lovers, such as kissing, hugging, and touching, though without a sexual dimension or motivation. This may be how an erotic transference in adult life finds its first inklings in the arms of mother: *When I am touched this way by you today, your warm affection recalls the love I experienced in my childhood with mother.* It can also work positively, healing a past in which our needs were not met, though we instinctively knew what they were: *When I am touched this way by you today, the warm affection goes back and heals the deficits and disappointments of my childhood experience with mother.*

In this same respect, the love we received in the past works forward in time and supports us now. When grandma showed us the five A's so reliably and warmly, she was implanting hardy resources of self-worth in us. She is still holding and comforting us as we—and so that we can—face life's challenges. Our ability to face the givens of life is constructed partially of her long-lasting touch. This is how the past indeed lives on and how love never ends.

In our clumsy rummaging around for connection, our needs for mirroring, idealizing, and twinship can also incorrectly appear to us as sexual desire. Our sexual intent may represent our long-standing yearning for a holding environment and for a trustworthy parent/partner. Just as our first opportunity to feel comfort was in the arms of mother, so our opportunity today may come from being held in the arms of a partner who provides the same unconditional nurturance.

Sex as Addiction

When we missed our chance for sexual explorations in high school, there is a chance that we may still seek sex in addictive or nonrelational ways, that is, in adolescent ways. Our failure at satisfaction in that arena shows us so clearly that we cannot make up for experiences we missed in the past. We can only lament the loss of what fit then and move on to what fits now.

We know we have advanced into adulthood when sex is no longer about sexual *activity* but about erotic/affectionate *energy*. Then the accent is not on a behavior that gives pleasure so much as on a loving force that shares it.

As healthy adults, our commitment to our partner in a marriage or serious relationship includes renunciation of other sexual liaisons. Unless we have agreed on an open marriage or relationship, our commitment is to monogamy. This means not only no outside sexual relationships but none in virtual reality—online. *Renunciation* is a difficult word in our freewheeling world, yet it is a spiritual practice in many traditions. For instance, in Buddhism it is recommended as an antidote to greed and craving. In that context renunciation does not refer to a repudiation of our natural instincts, only an ongoing custody over them so that our love relationship can be safeguarded. Sex is one of the many ways people find out the extent and seriousness of their commitment.

For some individuals, sex is also sometimes used to assist a fragile self in its attempts to stabilize. At a more profound level, we may be using sex to prevent fragmentation rather than for the relief of a personal drive or for mutual nurturance: We believe we will not be alive without *this*. However, a sense of self was not meant to come from that quarter. Robert Stolorow writes, "Sexualized attempts to compensate for voids and defects in the sense of self are meant to counteract fragmentation. . . . They are eroticized replacements for people who were traumatized through absent, disappointing, or unresponsive parents." The object of a sex addiction does not heal our wound but comforts and distracts us from our ongoing, often unacknowledged condition of emptiness.

Sex addiction can happen because of our terror of experiencing life as raw and real. We seek an escape, something by which we can transcend our predicament. Transcendence often seduces us away from reality (in the same way that "spiritual" explanations can be used to soften the blow of the givens of life rather than allowing a yes to their ruthless impact).

Regarding the phrase "raw and real," I share this humorous story. One night, I was lying in bed about to fall asleep when I was suddenly assailed with the bellowing shrieks of cats in heat outside my window. The poignant yowling was quite unnerving, but in the midst of this caterwauling a thought came to me. We humans might sound like that if we really expressed our sexual longings in a fully guttural way, uninhibited by our long history of politeness and propriety. There are natural sounds in us, probably never voiced, for all the feelings, pleasures, and aches that occur in our human sojourn. We keep the lid on our barbaric yelp, and I wonder at what cost? The cats tell it as it is for them, though they have no access to words. We have the *Oxford English Dictionary*, but it cannot give us even one primal scream, only words and words.

Love and In Love

"I want a girl just like the girl that married dear old Dad," the old song says. Indeed, relationship is more often reenactment than something truly new. What we see as the charms of this woman may be mostly her knack at arousing the familiar. We form close bonds with those who mimic our original caregivers. We somehow believe that mimicry offers us a guarantee: "This is the special person who will give me what I missed out on or once received or who will bring to an end my gnawing hunger for love."

The mute cells of our bodies gain a voice when we believe we will at last be loved as we always wanted to be. Here are two possible scenarios: Transference happens when we accept love here and now from someone but distrust it will be reliable because the love from our parents turned out not to be so. On the other hand, if love was reliable in childhood, we might expect it to be just that way with this new partner and be terribly disappointed if it turns out not to be so. We might even hold on to a partner as a flotation device when life's waters are rough, and not be interested in her at all when things calm down.

We are aware of the "chemistry" that happens between ourselves and someone else when we fall in love. Chemistry may not tell us about the rightness of a partner for us as much as about her rightness for setting up a repetition of our past. *What we call chemistry may be the unconscious recognition that we have found an apt candidate for transference.*

We might notice two kinds of chemistry. The healthy form of chemistry is a viscerally felt responsiveness that draws us to someone. It arises from interest and enthusiasm, and it includes some projection and transference. The addictive form of chemistry feels more like a restless compulsiveness that pulls us toward someone. It arises from neediness, fantasy-based projection, and merger transference in which the boundaries between ourselves and others overly blur.

Chemistry includes attraction to the physical look of someone. We know this is primarily based on a biological instinct. Physical attraction is also related to our belief that we have found someone who completes or mirrors us. The object of our affection seems to offer what we lack or to reflect what we deeply are. Finally, our attraction is a form of transference, since we imagine that pleasing looks make us a promise. We believe that "good-looking" will mean well-skilled in giving the five A's. Adults who investigate relationship candidates carefully will not be fooled by any of this. They will see external beauty as a dessert and inner beauty as the true source of nurturance.

In the romantic phase of a relationship, we may overlook some red flags and danger signals about that special someone who seems so suitable a candidate for healthy relating. It is an irony of psychology that we *have* to give up our accurate judgment long enough to let the necessary idealization/transference happen. Our blindness in love also makes the procreation of the human race more likely, which may be shrewd Mother Nature's real motive in keeping us unconscious. Later on in the relationship, however, we require a clear perception of reality so we can decide if we have found an appropriate nominee for a relationship commitment. What a confounding task: we have to let go of our full-spectrum vision to make contact and then we have to find it just in time to make the right commitment.

In romance, we idealize the other person, seeing total good where there is some good, seeing the answer to our prayers where there should be some doubt in our faith. We humans find our illusions immensely useful for creativity and self-soothing. On top of it all, fealty to the truth and to reality *have* to give way to imagination and illusion occasionally if we are to appreciate and be warmed by romance or poetry. Once again, we are in the garden of paradox, also called Eden.

Daring an Adult Love

Once a person knows a partner can be trusted, early memories of love or abuse within one's original family may come into focus for the first time or more clearly than ever before. Being loved brings up the past because we are reminded of what was once there or of what was always missing. The person who feels loved can love in return. He can also show his anger, longing, grief, excitement, and expectations. Abraham Maslow uses the phrase "safe enough to dare." We feel safe enough to risk showing our true feelings. Safety is an intelligent context for any venture, especially such a hazardous one as seeing a partner just as he is rather than as an artifact from the vault of our familiar past.

The presence of transference does not mean that our love is not real. As humans, we mostly relate in the present with one foot in the past. Love in an adult relationship makes the implicit explicit; archaic and forgotten longings are relocated in someone new. Indeed, the "in love" state recapitulates the ecstatic *fusion* we felt with our original caregivers. They held us so tenderly and made the perilous world so safe for us by the comforting warmth of their embraces. Or they did not hold us that way and we survived on wishes? We may be in love now either with what came to us or what we hoped for.

The healthy symbiotic phase of development in infancy, fusion of mother and child, recurs in adult romance. How can we be otherwise than ecstatic? At the same time, the original closeness might also have become threatening if it intruded upon our personal boundaries and felt claustrophobic. This is how the fear of engulfment may have originated. We bring that fear with us as we enter an intimate relationship. We are watching out for the danger of being crushed while welcoming the clinch. When we create relationships of both closeness and distance, we are simply maintaining our own original safety measures while trying to be intimate too. Everything about us seems to move toward reconciling apparent contradictions, ultimately a spiritual enterprise.

However, some of us were never safe enough with our parents to form basic trust, so we have minimal capacity for commitment in an adult relationship. We keep waiting for the other shoe to drop, fearing that after the clinches will come abandonment. If that was the progression in childhood, we are likely to expect a replay today. We might even choose the kind of partner who will repeat the betrayals or whom we will be able to train to do so.

Romeo's "I want you" was total. For us, it may be fraught with ambivalence. "I want you *and* I am afraid." That fear may read out as "Don't get too close and don't try to make me stay." On the other hand, fearless enthusiasm for becoming more conscious may sound this way: "My hesitancy about letting you get close to me helps me notice where my work is, and I intend to do it by confronting my fear." The sign of a healthy relationship is one in which the ambivalence is recognized and does not cause alarm or escape. It is noticed, admitted, and worked with.

The question then arises, are we staying with our relationship because we are really into it or because it is our style to stick to our commitments? "I gave my word and I intend to stand by it" is not a commitment to the relationship but to one's own standards. A real commitment is renewed daily because we still believe it reflects our love for the other as well as our own deepest needs and wishes. There are no white knuckles, only warm hands that hold each other in the light and in the dark.

It is important to notice that as we grow and as we become healthier, our needs change. The original reasons we came together may no longer obtain. Our relationship evolves best as we notice our authentic needs, state them, and negotiate ever new ways of having them met. A simple example makes this clear: Our son once needed us to change his diapers; now he needs us to loan him money for a down payment on a house. We move with the times when we love.

In the following example, Roy and Tess exhibit that mysterious combination of fear of abandonment and fear of engulfment that characterize so many troubled relationships.

Tess realizes, "I want more than Roy is willing to give." This is a tip-off to the presence of two fears in one relationship: Tess fears abandonment and Roy fears engulfment. Roy needs space and time alone, and Tess has trouble allowing it without feeling insecure. She suspects he has secrets, and she wishes he would share as much about himself as she shares about herself. Roy has learned to keep secrets as a way of maintaining privacy. Questions feel intrusive and make him angry.

Roy takes Tess for granted and even feels entitled to be taken care of by Tess, which she does willingly. But it feels to Roy that she is overdoing it, and her clinging and closeness makes him pull away even more. To make up for the guilt she feels about not being enough for Roy, Tess allows him to be in full control. His preferences take precedence over hers and he makes all the major decisions. Roy has lost respect for Tess because of this, but it would scare him even more if she took a stand as an equal.

Tess is needy for affection but afraid of receiving it. Otherwise, why be with Roy? Her neediness leads her to equate sex with affection. Roy enjoys sex with Tess, because he has learned how to engage in it athletically without having to bond more intimately through it. It would frighten him to be truly sexually intimate and have sex lead to bonding beyond his control.

Tess rationalizes. She makes excuses for his distancing and her coping. Roy intellectualizes. He explains away his feelings and fears. Tess shows her fear of losing Roy but not her fear of having a relationship that works. She does not show her anger, because that might jeopardize what little she has. Roy shows his anger but not his fear. To show fear to someone who cares means you might be held too long in her arms.

Tess feels insecure in her relationship with Roy, but it is all familiar from her childhood home life. Her father was emotionally distant and her mother was only intermittently available. Tess never experienced the five A's from either of them. Though both parents seemed to offer love, neither could be trusted to follow through.

Roy was brought up as a little prince with all his needs met and with no obligation to give in return. A darling needs no reassurance later, only acknowledgment of his entitlements. At the same time, little Roy was surrounded by women who fussed over him and overly clasped him in their own needy arms. This may be why Roy asks that Tess stay put while he comes and goes at will. He comes and goes often, because too much time together feels suffocating. Roy knows very well that time together leads to firmer bonding, which will call for a more adult commitment, another surrender of control.

Both Tess and Roy blame Tess. She believes it is her fault that Roy is the way he is. She has not learned that Roy was programmed this way long ago. Roy sees Tess as a burdensome, demanding partner. He does not realize that Tess is acting out of cellular programming and unconscious transferences much of the time.

Neither partner is to blame, nor can either change within the present pattern. Change can happen only when each works through the original fears and hurts that have been smuggled into their relationship from households of the distant past.

Tess has abandoned herself, just as she was abandoned in childhood and is being abandoned by Roy now. In her father transference she is doing to herself what was done to her. She has hired just the right actor to play the part of her father in her drama. Roy is guarding himself from the possibility that anyone else will engulf him as happened to him in childhood. In so doing, he is abandoning his chance at changing. Both have lost touch with the excitement of stepping out of character, of acting as if they were unafraid and thereby discovering how fear finally fades.

Roy operates out of a deep bias against women—a misogyny. Ironically, he is hiding the very quality that would increase his lovability. It thus becomes a self-fulfilling prophecy: "Women cannot be trusted to love me appropriately. Since women cannot be trusted, I need to hide my softer side and distance my partner, who eventually rejects me and thereby proves I was right about women's untrustworthiness!" Over-protectiveness by a parent will be felt by a child as rejection since it cancels his right to personal freedom. Roy knew this, deep down, all his life. "Deep down" means unconscious and yet alive in conscious life.

Roy has some things in his favor: his charm, his good looks, his financial stability. These make him appealing in so many ways that he can get by without having to be intimate. His assets promise a lot and make life so comfortable. His relationship may last if Tess remains willing to play out her pain with him, or if she resigns herself to go on living without the focused commitment that men like Roy can never deliver. Ironically, Tess is the partner in this relationship most likely to leave. She may secretly line up a backup partner when Roy's withdrawal and distancing become intolerable. Roy will then be reinforced in his mistrust of women and inaugurate the cycle again with her or with a new partner—as will Tess.

Working Out Our Relationship Clashes

"It's not just you and me transacting here, but each of us is transacting with his parents through the other. This whole hassle has been about getting over what happened to us in childhood."
—a client's comment to her partner during a counseling session

We keep believing that repetition of the past will clear things up, when all that really does it is clearly looking at the situation with full responsibility for the leftover tears it calls on us to shed. Our wounds become gateways when we dare to enter them through grief work. Courage happens as a result of this daring. As Jung says, "If there is a fear of falling, the only safety is in deliberately jumping." Maintaining an unconscious transference keeps us standing on the cliff, not even daring to look at the waters below.

Transference happens in ever more complex ways as a relationship becomes serious. In fact, getting serious may mean that transference has kicked in and is proceeding, as it always does, unconsciously. A light relationship can be defined as one with minimal transference.

Freud wrote, "Every conflict has to be fought out in the sphere of transference . . . for when all is said and done it is impossible to destroy anyone in absentia or in effigy." We cannot get to our parents now, but we can be aggressive toward our near and dear. Perhaps the addictive violence characterizing our society is somehow an enactment of just such transference. We react toward the collective based on what is personal.

Here is an example of how transference may appear in a conflict. A wife acts as a caretaker to her husband and he shows appreciation and does not quite notice that she is ultimately controlling. The caretaker is imitating her controlling/caretaking mother. The husband being controlled believes, "This woman makes life easy for me and must really love me because she does so much for me." In his childhood, love was shown by his mother's constant caretaking of him, and a dependency resulted. Neither partner notices how he or she may perpetuate the past. When an adult relationship places us in familiar surroundings, we may feel so safe and comfortable that we lose our critical sense of what is really going on.

Here is another example: A partner scolds his male lover and thereby sounds like that man's dad. He bristles because he still hates being told what to do and told who he is. This triggers anger, but it is aimed at both a father and a partner, and perhaps a former partner too. This is why our feelings can become so dramatic and tangled. They seldom emerge in their pure form in our relationships, since no relationship is purely between two people. At least four are in the room most of the time.

Our transference-rich feelings are saturated with story lines, concepts, and mind-sets. Our raw healthy feelings, on the other hand, simply flow as they are without censorious judgments. Anger attached to a transference is not simply displeasure at a perceived injustice but usually picks up elements of judgment, blame, and demand that the partner change— familiar from the anger of a parent toward us in our childhood. When we contact our feelings through such coatings of ego, we can guess that more is happening than the issue we are facing. In another instance, we may feel sad and grieve about a partner leaving us. But in transference we might add painful layers of how what made us sad was also insult, rejection, betrayal, or abandonment. These sensitive overlays are clues to what we felt in our childhood transactions with our parents or other significant adults. Unfortunately, they more often become transferences than areas that are addressed and cleared.

How Codependency Arises

The work is certainly to make use of the transference, but then to take action in the immediate situation. We may stay too long in what does not work, that is, become codependent. We may keep trying to fix a spouse. We may keep being patient with his trespasses against our boundaries or those of our children. The struggle to adjust to a relationship that is dysfunctional or hurtful is not as useful as the struggle to decide what to do. The decision is the same as working with transference itself, to address the issue so it can be worked through and so change can result.

A partner who refuses to join us in this but simply continues in his dysfunction or abuse is no longer a partner but a threat to our well-being. This is where our fear can become a trap that paralyzes us further or a signal that it is time to set ourselves free. We do ourselves the best favor when we look at our ring and ask if it is a memory symbol, a real symbol, or a handcuff. Then from deep within we might summon up the meaning in the hymn of our childhood, "Let freedom ring."

Codependency is a term coined originally to refer to the partner of an alcoholic; it was intended to show that alcoholism is a family/relationship disease. The nondrinking partner enables the other to continue in his addiction by making excuses for him and by staying with him despite his abuse. In bygone eras, to stay in this kind of relationship was considered a sign of love and personal strength; to break off the relationship or to move out would have been considered selfish.

Using the term *codependency* to denote a problem in us provides a bridge into a new and healthier way of seeing what love is about. To put up with abuse, to stay in a painful situation with no prospect of change for the better, is loyalty but not love. It is harmful to both parties. To see it this way, we have to believe that we have a right to happiness, a cause and result of self-esteem. We have to believe that love is a two-way street, a cause and result of healthy intimacy. We have to believe that unconditional love does not mean being unconditionally committed to staying stuck. (This more mature understanding of love is a cause and result of balanced living.)

Thus the term *codependency* revolutionized love and set us free from a vision of life as endurance. Now we can see that life is about sharing, not only giving. It is about love that includes being happy. This is not really new. It was always part of the wisdom in the collective human psyche. Hence the poet Sir John Suckling penned the following lines in the seventeenth century:

> *To have loved alone will not suffice*
> *Unless we also have been wise*
> *And have our loves enjoyed.*

Practice
Committing to Loving-kindness

We may notice the telltale signs of ego when we react *against* our partner: We are trying to build a case against the other person, blaming him, condemning him, defending our position, refusing to hear his legitimate feedback to us, wanting to retaliate. The signs of ego when we move *toward* someone include neediness, insistence that the other meet our expectations, attempts to use the other to offset our own loneliness or as an escape from doing our own work on ourselves.

It is a relationship task to work with transferences from our partner onto us. The practice is listening with the openness of the five A's while noticing the mind-sets of the other without censure. We do not become so aroused that we have to react in kind. We feel the pain in those compulsive habits of the ego. We can focus our attention on becoming open to the other in loving-kindness and in being assertive at the same time.

We can then practice showing healthy anger when we feel abused. We can practice noticing negative reactions to us without blame or retaliation. In the ego world, revenge is meant to restore balance after an injustice. To seek balance using loving-kindness is a truly humane project and a mighty spiritual feat. Love becomes real for us once we keep no accounts of the wrongs done to us. This can become a commitment that we make within an intimate relationship.

As a practice, say to your partner, "I am making a commitment never to retaliate against you in any way no matter what you do." You may also make a gift of this commitment and write it on a card or valentine. Notice if you have any resistance to this idea. Notice if you inwardly insist that your partner has to do the same for you, an unnecessary gesture if you really mean what you are saying. You may also extend your commitment to include an end to sarcasm, ridicule, comebacks, teasing, or any other passive-aggressive behaviors. Your resistance to making such a commitment certainly provides you important information about the nature of your ego and the scope of your love.

Practice
Entering Another's World

The practice of free-floating attentiveness is a starting point for this practice. Our most skillful response to others' reactions to us is not to react in like ways but rather to *enter the other's world.* We simply open to what we see, with no attempt to stop, correct, or battle it. As long as we want to "set the record straight" about ourselves or show that we are definitely "right," communication is in jeopardy because our main purpose is to establish control rather than to be open. The two spiritually mature alternative practices include (1) no longer correcting impressions of us and (2) summoning up the compassion that can most easily lead to loving-kindness. Compassion is generally from us toward others. Loving-kindness extends into the great compassion that widens so that is aimed toward ourselves, others, and the world.

We may have noticed a spouse's transference before she does. We may likewise notice what our partner is not ready to know. In this instance, the way of compassion is to proceed slowly, in honor of her timing. We may also have to be prepared for an angry reaction from her for our having dared to catch her in her transferences. She may not be grateful to see where her work is but may defend herself with a hostile reply and then distrust or resent us later. This transference resistance and projection makes intimate contact quite impossible until everyone calms down. When ego fears are aroused, we do well to back off for a while.

We may also misinterpret someone's behavior. Themes in comedies of mistaken identity portray humorous examples of transference but also certainly show how the visible and tangible do not tell the whole story. There is a hidden meaning behind appearances. *In a truly intimate relationship, each person wants to be found in that deep meaning.* It takes humility on our part to bow to the mystery of the other rather than to believe we know her like a book. Then knowledge gives way to wisdom. To bow is to bend our ego toward a higher power than itself. Perhaps it would help to practice bowing more often around the house.

> *In Zen practice one bows to the Buddha principle, the imminence of awakening within ourselves. . . . A bow is a wonderful way to pay attention to the world around you.*
> —Peter Matthiessen

12

Noticing Transferences in Our Relationships

Every state of being in love reproduces infantile prototypes. The discovery of a love object is, in effect, a re-discovery.
—Sigmund Freud

Communications within our primary relationship become clearer and more effective when we acknowledge the transference dimension in our arguments with each other: "I see my mother in you, and extracting her from you is what I have to work on." This admission can make the difference between working something out and letting it cascade into ongoing resentment. Our parents and former partners are phantom presences in every dispute. Can we call them by name rather than name-calling our partner?

We confront our own transference issues not only by identifying their origin but by presenting our needs more consciously and wholesomely to our partner. We show our feelings, declare our hidden wishes, and state our expectations directly to the new person. Then she no longer represents the past person, and we no longer live in the past tense.

As we finally come to know our real needs, disentangled from so many transferences, we might take a second look at our partner and perhaps

wonder if she ever really can fulfill them. This is an important—and perhaps perilous—moment in a relationship when new negotiations can
begin or a breakup can result. Our task is to ask for what we need or to
reconcile ourselves to our partner's limited capacity to fulfill us. We can
work in therapy to see if change is possible. We can look at how we both
contribute to the inadequacy. If everything fails, we might ask if *anyone*
can fulfill such needs as we have? Maybe the minimal dividend from our
partner is a fair exchange for the company of someone we love so much.
Then we are challenged to find ways to make up for the lack by fulfilling
ourselves.

When we are caught in cycles of transference, no events are totally new.
The opportunity for new experiences happens when we work through our
transferences by making them conscious and venturing a new trajectory
of behavior and reactions. We can begin by saying to ourselves, "This is
happening now, not then." Such placing of ourselves in the correct time
zone has the effect of centering us. We then operate from a grounded now,
not from the shifting sands of then.

Practice
Letting Conflicts Help Us

Here is an example and a practice that shows how recognizing the transference element of a relationship issue helps both partners. In childhood
we were often misunderstood. Now we become incensed when our partner misunderstands our motives. This overreaction may mean that being
misunderstood is still in its "back then" form. We are not simply feeling
it now as a new event. By diving into its bodily felt sense, our issue with
being misunderstood can be traced back to how it came through in the
past as abandonment. That evokes the terror of being disconnected, and
that is what we feel now when we are misunderstood, hence its heftiness
to us.

Disruptions and conflicts in our adult relationships can facilitate the
working through of our transferences. This is because, like great plays and
films, they dramatically evoke or perpetuate our original tensions with

our parents. Once this happens, we can say, perhaps aloud, "Oh, this is exactly what I felt in childhood. I am an adult now. This woman is not my mother. What is my adult response?" To commit ourselves to address, process, resolve, and integrate our feelings in ways like that helps us work through the illusion of past-in-present.

We can say to ourselves, "I am not being understood, and that does not have to mean that I am being deserted." Part of this practice is finding that our antennae regarding being misunderstood have become more acute over the years. Now we may wonder if it has become easier to stay stuck in the myth that we are cursed to be misunderstood rather than to feel the full weight of our core abandonment. Our focus on the red herring was a defense against our authentic feeling.

We can practice daring affirmations like these:

I lighten my desperate need to be understood.
I let go of my fear of being misunderstood.
I am content with how it comes out rather than only content if it
        comes out my way.

In any case, the need to be understood is legitimate, though the givens of life do not necessarily permit fulfillment. True maturation in intimacy consists not in leaving needs behind but rather in three achievements:

1. We grieve what was missing of the five A's in our past. Thus the work begins with the challenge to restore or establish a bond after grieving what disrupted it in our past, either in childhood or in former relationships. This direct approach liberates us from our compulsion to misdirect our past into unconscious transferences, which so crookedly attempt to make us whole.

2. We recruit supportive others who can give us age-appropriate and healthy mirroring and we become open to receiving it from any quarter. We notice that no one is perfect in providing all that we need, so we reconcile our ourselves to the human dose. This is a yes to humanity as it is.

3. We appreciate all that we do receive from the one we love, and this leads us to give the five A's in return.

In love, the gates of my soul spring open, allowing me to breathe a new air of freedom and forget my own petty self. In love, my whole being streams forth out of the rigid confines of narrowness and self-assertion that make me a prisoner of my own poverty and emptiness.
—Karl Rahner

Good-Enough Relating

Freud spoke of a "shared love of truth" in the therapist-patient relationship that expunges the past from the present. In an adult bond, partners have noticed how they transfer onto each other and are working on whatever past issue still interferes with the possibility of an authentic you-and-I relationship. Transference, like the past, never vanishes entirely. A real relationship happens when there are more you-and-I moments than there are transference moments. This happens when the observing ego can step back and reflect on transference without giving in to it.

The psychologist D. W. Winnicott famously asserted that all we need in childhood is a "good enough mothering." Our mothers don't have to be perfectly attuned to us 100 percent of the time in order for us to develop into well-adjusted children and adults. We only need her to show us the five A's more often than not. Likewise in relationships, we don't have to strive for perfection, but we can talk about "good enough relating" to our intimate partners, family, and friends. When we acknowledge ongoing transference in daily life and allow a greater frequency of you-and I moments, this is good-enough relating. We do not have to clear out the past completely, nor can we. It is part of us and adds color and richness to our lives as well as preserving a sense of our continuity. Achieving total separation from the past would be like burning the family album so we could make room for the newspaper.

With Emily Dickinson, in her poem, "I'm ceded, I've stopped being theirs" we can go on recalling childhood:

But this time—Adequate—Erect,
With Will to choose, or to reject. . . .

We now see that working through our transferences is the same as equipping ourselves for healthy relationships. At the same time, we are becoming clearer about who we are, how our past influences us, and how we can grow from it. This is how we find more than one chance at a happy childhood. This is how we finally empty the kettle on the back burner. We can become comfortable in our freedom from constricting ties to back-then, and content in our relating to others here-now. The move away from transference is toward mindfulness.

It is now clear that relating to significant others is a dialogue between our unconscious and their unconscious. The possibility of you-and-I relating opens up once what has been unconscious/implicit becomes conscious/explicit. This working through of the transference does not happen all at once or once and for all. It is, like life itself, a continual process, not a manufactured product; a journey, not a done deal.

Most of us would say that we want to let go of being under the influence of transference so we can live entirely in a you-and-I relationship. Yet, many of us have a resistance to the nonstop intimacy this would entail, even if it were possible. If our trust in ourselves, in others, or in relationships is still uncertain or lacking, it will be scary to let go of our transferences and projections long enough to let someone into our lives in the totality of who he or she is. We will make sure no one is new; candidates for relationship with us will have to be facsimiles.

Yet we have it in us to be patient and compassionate toward ourselves for the time it takes to look directly and behold a truly new face. We are not geared to see anything or anyone fully and permanently anyway. This could be why they told us in childhood that it was impolite to stare. This could be why religion and mythology teach that we cannot look at God and live. The beatific vision was reserved for after death: "We see now through a glass darkly, but [only] then face to face" (1 Cor. 13:12).

It is also important to remind ourselves that transference does not always require dissolving. Transference happens in a positive way when we link a partner to benevolent figures from the past and find comfort in his presence by reason of the similarity. The comforting trust, established within the holding environment of the five A's, aids in the building of an adult intimate commitment. We live in the present without anachronisms but with cherished memories that have now been beneficially revived.

The Introvert/Extrovert Dimension in Relating

We sometimes become accustomed to a level of engagement from a partner that may be inadequate to our needs. A you-and-I relationship has an engaged focus, not all the time but certainly when interacting seriously. A partner who rarely listens or who glazes over when we talk about ourselves is not really available for intimacy. A long history with such an absentee partner may make us gloss over his narcissistic unavailability. This is the equivalent of demeaning our own needs for intimacy. We have to ask if we are colluding in the pain of not being heard, begun in childhood, repeated now.

We might confuse a narcissist with an introvert, since both can seem cold or distant. They are not the same. It may be difficult for an introvert to provide an engaged focus in an intimate relationship. It seems to the other that he is absent or not available when in reality he needs space in order to be ready to show closeness in his own way. We have to look into what the other is really up to and appreciate, as well as become used to, the peculiar brand of his love. Everyone loves, but not in a way we might recognize if our version of love is based on how we show, want, or remember it. To be loved requires an openness to new brands of kisses.

Introverts cannot let in too much of the world or the impact of others' presence. They usually feel depleted by contact, even when it seems minimal. An extrovert partner may be angry that the introvert is depleted. Some extroverts may take in too much and feel stressed. They are animated by contact, but sometimes lose their sense of boundaries in the process. An introvert sets boundaries on how much he will take in, but sometimes with more rigidity than is necessary to safeguard his security. An extrovert is much more open, but sometimes has fewer boundaries than are necessary to ensure his serenity.

The introvert/extrovert distinction helps us see how we might be over- or under-incorporating, not taking enough in or taking in too much from others and the world around us:

Shutting out too much:	*Opening to an extreme:*
The other makes no impact or turns us off	*We let the other come at us too strongly*
We fall asleep or zone out while the other is talking	We are overstimulated by the other's presence
We are bored, distracted, and disengaged	We are so fascinated that we lose sight of anything else
We are indifferent	We are obsessed
We easily or inappropriately become irritable in the company of the other	We make allowances for the other no matter how difficult he may be to endure
We forget appointments	We are overly excited by the thought of seeing the other
We begin our visits late or end them early	We cannot get enough of the other
We feel or show contempt or impatience	We strongly admire the other even when he does not deserve it
We cannot empathize with the other, nor are we willing to put effort into it	We experience a form of folie à deux, feeling what the other feels and losing our own sense of individuality
We forget important information about or from the other	We recall every detail of the other's life
We miss cues	We notice everything
We do not strongly or sincerely care what may happen to the other	We have rescue fantasies
We are on guard against closeness	We are overly familiar
We have little or no interest in the other's experiences, especially inner experience	We make inappropriate inquiries into the other's private business
Feelings are not evoked	We are flooded with feelings
All this adds up to under-incorporating: not letting enough in.	*All this adds up to over-incorporating: letting in too much.*

This list also applies to therapists' reactions to clients in countertransference.

Both over- and under-incorporation are boundary issues, shifting from disregard of personal space to honoring space and the inner core of each other. The healthy alternative is a continual cycling of closeness and distance, always shown with respect. Healthy people have what infants are born with: a stimulus barrier, an instinctive shutting off of unwanted stimulation without breaking the connection with the other. This is an alternative to dissociation from or rejection of the other. Rejection may also take the forms of sarcasm or teasing. Healthy humor brings surprise followed by delight. Sarcasm and teasing bring surprise followed by pain. These are passive—and hurtful—ways of setting boundaries on how close or intimate we will allow the other to be.

When we fear abandonment by the other, we might compromise our boundaries so that we lose our self-respect. When we fear engulfment by the other, we might tighten our boundaries so much that love cannot easily flourish. An infant crawling, falling, bumping into objects is gaining a sense of boundaries. Can we see failures and hard knocks as helping us now in that same way?

Working Back in Time

Though we see ourselves as adults of a certain age, we contain within ourselves all of our former ages. I still know the times tables exactly as I learned them at my elementary school, the Skinner School in the 1940s, and deep down I am in many ways still the child who went there. In fact, I looked at my fourth-grade report card a few years ago and the comments on my behavior and attitude precisely reflected the traits in my personality now! Mrs. Williams had defined my personality quite perfectly. I am still that kid in so many ways. This may explain the fact that I often feel like a child around Mom now, even when she does nothing to trigger me. Just the presence or voice of Mother is enough to reinstitute the old transactions with her. What a proof of the longevity of transference!

We may have been suspicious of the love offered to us by our controlling mother or the love we were told was there for us but was certainly not shown by our distant father. In an adult relationship we may be with a partner who loves us without engulfing us, thus reversing our mother imago, the inner image and meaning we carry of her. This partner also acts lovingly but without declaring it, recasting our father imago. Now, paradoxically, two things happen. We let love in and we trust love whether or not it is spoken. The dangerous love from mother and the doubted love from father are remembered, but they become less impactful on us. We notice then that we feel less anger or fear as we let go of blame of our parents while still remaining aware of their accountability. This heals the memory, that is, works back in time.

The healing of a memory is the same as releasing us from the need to transfer something onto others. This is because what was dangerous before has now become safe, so the past no longer holds us back from new ways of relating. We are not so rushed into transference, because the past has been laid to rest.

Being loved by a trustworthy partner is thus one of the ways resolution happens. Now we can let love in without the fear of being engulfed, and that makes gestures associated with mother's smothering in the past less influential in our present intimate relationship. We can let love in with more trust that we will not be abandoned soon after, and that works back to make father's absence less traumatic when we recall it now.

Shakespeare said, "Love's not time's fool."

We can add, "Let love be time's repair."

We Really Can Be Here Now

The frequency of transference rearing its head in relationships convinces us that our interactions are not always adult here-and-now enterprises. This need not discourage us, because we can learn the practice of mindful consciousness that leads us to know our parental or former relationship transferences.

Here is an example of how it can happen: At a party, your partner is spending an inordinate amount of time with another woman. You can see how attentive he is to her and you have not recently seen that intensity in his way of being with you. You are enraged at him because you see this as insulting and even as a form of infidelity. Actually, however, what is happening in you is much more unsophisticated. The child within you is not using words like *infidelity*. She is crying out, "Oh, he likes her more than me. I want him to like me more than her." Or it may be even more hard-hitting: "Oh, now I see I will never be loved the way I want." That is how we sounded in fourth grade when something like this happened to us. We were much more in touch with our real feelings then and we told them to ourselves just as they were. (Nonetheless, even in fourth grade we were perhaps remembering what we felt when our brother was born and all the attention was diverted to him. Yes, even that early we were experiencing transference reactions.)

A useful and perhaps embarrassing—that is, ego-dismantling—practice is to speak to ourselves about what happens to us in our relationships *in fourth-grade words,* as in the examples above. This is a bottom-line-honest wording of our experience that helps us see the primal depth of our need and of its consequent transference. Then we understand what our fear-and-blame reaction is really about and we take responsibility for how we are transferring past to present, parent to partner, former partner to new partner. When we rebuke ourselves for sounding childish, we may be missing out on a valuable resource.

Of course, our party story does not end here. After the ball is over, you can say to your partner, without blaming, that it hurt to feel you were being pushed aside, that you know part of the hurt was your own transference, but that nonetheless you want an agreement that he be more conscious of your feelings at future parties by sharing more of his time with you. That combination of assertiveness, responsibility, and humility is how we work on ourselves and on our relationships at the same time.

We can alter our story slightly to see just how our inner world can become a personal holding environment in which our life events and experiences can be felt, processed, and worked through, before we confront our partner. For instance, a woman suspects her partner of excessive or inappropriate intimacy toward one of her coworkers. If she can contain the feelings within herself and let them speak their truth to her, she is less likely to jump into a dramatic reaction.

When we learn to pause, allowing an inner sense of space around a relationship event, we are able to perceive meanings that an immediate reaction does not allow us to see. In addition, this holding of the fact in the container of our secret self makes us more trusting of ourselves. We grow in the very strength that will make it possible to confront our partner, when the time is right, in exactly the ways that work.

Practice
Pausing to Check In and Settle In

We can only work effectively with difficult relationship issues when we know how to calm down. How can we prepare our inner self for calm openness? Here is a practice:

1. We practice *pausing* between stimulus and response, the essence of freedom.
2. *We can feel* what we feel fully before acting on it.
3. *We check in with our bodily reactions.* We ask, "Where do I feel this and how does it impact my body?" This is useful because it gives us information that the mind cannot put into words.
4. *We can notice* our feelings mindfully rather than becoming trapped in the habitual mind-sets of ego: judgment, control, defensiveness, attachment to an outcome, the need to be right, and the fear of facing the truth of what might be happening. All of these are refusals to accept reality as it is and others as they are.
5. *We can respect* the timing an event requires before making it into an issue with someone else.
6. *We can cease presuming* we know what others are up to. We can make an attempt to think up three or more explanations as alternatives to what came to us as a first impression or our conclusion about what someone said or did. We often see only someone's behavior and jump to our favorite explanatory story. Realizing there are many possible stories may liberate us from patterns of presumption, which happens when there are no such options.
7. *We can go with the flow* of events with free-floating attention, that is, a listening or witnessing attitude. This dismisses our ego

from center stage. Indeed, going with the flow is a way of letting go of ego. This is because our ego is a set of embedded, habitual, and highly conditioned reactions. Our ego is out of work when we become less focused on our own entitlements, less reactive to specific events, less fixated on what is stuck in our craw. We find the serenity of green pastures and still waters. The fall of ego's empire leads to an awakening into a heavenly world where the lion of control finally lies down with the lamb of let-it-be.

8. *Mindfulness is the final step.* The mind-sets of ego are projections. They are forms of entertainment to the mind in need of drama rather than presence. The mind-sets of ego thrill the mind with faux feelings rather than open an accepting space as mindfulness does. To transcend ego in relationship is to let go of these mind-sets, since they represent identifications with the story of right and wrong, fear and desire, control and illusion.

"Identification" means that we mistakenly believe that our thoughts and emotions are us, rather than mental constructions that have us in their grip. Mindfulness meditation helps us loosen that grip so that we can look past our habitual mind-sets into the moment-by-moment kaleidoscope of reality. Then we do not promote our thoughts to any higher status than that given to floats that pass us in a parade. We notice we can be aware in a new way in moments that transcend discursive thought: our attention is penetrating and direct since it is no longer mediated by words or syllogisms. Thoughts are ornaments; mindfulness is the tree of emancipation from externals, another word for enlightenment. We have lightened up and lighted up our minds.

In mindfulness, our mind-sets are called by name and no longer entertained. Then we are present to ourselves and others in dedicated loyalty to the now: as-I-am, as-you-are, as-it-is. We are no longer conditioned by our beliefs, projections, and expectations. We reach into the unmanifested reality, the immortal diamond no-self that transcends the conditioned ego world. Authentic love can only happen in this diamond essence of egolessness. The reason the inflated mind-beset ego cannot love is because it cannot tolerate that diamond essence, so it—tragically—breaks contact with love's very origin.

In his poem "Poetry of Departures," Philip Larkin uses the phrase "an audacious, purifying, elemental move." The most courageous step is no longer to live by ego entitlements and demands but in full dedication to real and loving presence. The practices in this book may help get us there. Grace does the rest.

Sometimes it happens that we receive the power to say yes to ourselves, that peace enters into us and makes us whole, that self-hate and self-contempt disappear, and that our self is reunited with itself. Then we can say that grace has come upon us.
—Paul Tillich

13

From Transference to Transformation

Sustained empathic inquiry . . . leads to uncovering the client's unconscious organizing principles and then making them accessible to transformation.

—Robert Stolorow

Our Psychological Work

Transference helps us grow when it exchanges the role of casting director for that of prompter. We stop setting the stage and lining up the actors. Instead, we look at the stage we have set and the actors we have hired, and let it all prompt us to recall our lines: "This drama is designed by me in accord with my past. Now I can let it become my prompter, helping me speak my truth in the moment."

As consciousness grows, transference comes to light and loses its power to determine our present life as once it did. Then, as Freud says, "Transference the obstacle . . . becomes transference the ally." We realize that in most of our relationships we have been seeing reflections, and we make the choice to pass through the looking glass to the reality of who others really are and can be. This is how transference can become transformation.

Heinz Kohut uses the expression "the crucible of transference." This phrase reflects the painful and yet richly alchemical process by which we recover from our misrepresentations. The long-lasting experiences of childhood can become grist for the mill of transformation. Then the lead of transference becomes the gold of self-realization.

Freud, speaking of transference in therapy, said that not working with transference is like successfully summoning a spirit from the dead and not asking it a question. We can learn to make sense of our immediate reality by using or evoking a past prototype. This is because we are always editing past memories and experiences in accord with our unconscious fantasies and then transferring them onto the present. We can take advantage of this penchant in our psyche and let it help us work through our issues. Our task is not hasty burial but careful exhumation to examine what really happened. Only then can proper burial proceed.

In working through transference, we separate projections from reality and we individualize persons rather than seeing them as facsimiles or archetypes. This is the crowning achievement of our psychological work on transference. That work shifts life from something that happens to something that opens. A space opens in us in the sense that now we see that we do not have to remain stuck in old beliefs or caught in imprisoning compulsions. Transference becomes its literal meaning, *carrying us over* the thresholds that lead to resolving our enigmatic past.

In psychoanalysis, interpretation of transference is the main tool by which insight into behavior helps effect a change. In Buddhism insight is considered to be a path out of suffering. Insight/consciousness is not simply a mental achievement. It is also a deeply cellular, sense-filled way of grasping reality. It is not like knowing geography. It is like knowing the stove is hot by touching it, knowing the rose is fragrant by smelling it, knowing losing someone can hurt long after it happens.

Consciousness happens when our inner trio plays its tune: our head knows; our heart feels; our gut agrees. We have to know at the gut level that we are treating another person as we wanted to treat our father. At the same time, we do not lose sight of the fact that others are indeed always more than themselves. They do make our old relations come back in new vesture; they are reflections of age-old human archetypes; they are shadow figures of our own disowned selves. So we acknowledge that transference never fully disappears, nor does it need to. The past cannot be killed off, but it can lose weight. Gradually, we notice we can let go of attachment to our past ("attachment to the past" being another description of transference). The "powers that be" can become the powers that have been. When they exist only in mental memory, they do not complicate our relationships or hurt us. Adhesiveness is what hurts. In our work on transference we attempt to undo the adhesions between past and present. We are then able to redo our way of relating so that we can have an airy, novel, spacious experience of someone. We make room for the reality of who others are in themselves.

Practice
A Checklist

The practices so far have helped us work through our transferences by addressing, processing, resolving, and integrating them and the issues that underlie them. The following is a list of qualities that appear when an issue in transference has been as fully resolved and integrated as it can be. Use it as a checklist to determine how much of what you have worked on so far in the practices has been implemented and completed:

- The memory remains but its impact keeps reducing over time. If it began as a ten on the one-to-ten scale, we now notice it has dropped below a five, and that it remains below the midpoint. If it occasionally spikes back up toward ten, it does not remain there for long but returns to its new set point, which also keeps lowering with time.
- The thought of what happened returns to us in a new internal context. It is one of spaciousness rather than crowdedness or collapse. It is no longer the sudden swoop of a pterodactyl upon us but the passing over of a curious, but not hungry falcon.
- We no longer have to act out our unskillful behavior. For instance, we can admit we want to run but not let our feet join in. We can report a feeling to a partner rather than avoid it or reenter an old pattern that harms the relationship. We are not compelled; we have a choice.
- Our wound now seems to help us. We feel stronger for having lived through it. Painful home events have become like spiders in the eaves. We coexist, with some sense of mutual benefit, though it would also be all right if they departed.

- The issue passes through us differently. Before it was Godzilla destroying the landscape and Bambi too. Now he lumbers through our inner jungle more courteously, and we are not damaged or frightened by his appearance. The issue or personal imago from our past resides in us not as a crushing blow but as a mild fact. The issue does not damage our serenity, our relationships, or our work. In other words, it no longer interferes with or determines how we live our lives or how we show our love.
- Any wish for retaliation against those who may have hurt us has passed away. Retaliation against ourselves in the form of nagging guilt or futile regret has significantly diminished or vanished altogether.
- We see some humor in our transference and in our reactions to it.
- Serenity and equanimity have become more important to us than ever. We want tranquillity of mind not hysterics, chaos, or drama in our relationships. Free of the emotional jumble caused by projection and transference, we notice a space opening up from deep inside us. This is our pure identity beyond any story. In that spaciousness, we begin to make choices that lead to fewer encumbrances and no entanglements.
- We put less accent on what happens and more accent on how we hold what happens. We are no longer trying to be in control of life's unavoidable challenges or givens, nor to head them off lest they make us feel something. We trust that we will be able to handle whatever comes our way. Fear has become yes.
- We are more compassionate toward those who transfer onto us, and we find it easier to practice loving-kindness.

How Spiritual Practice Renews Us

Spiritual practice is a complement to our psychological work. We begin by exploring how spirituality may help us.

In Buddhist psychology clear seeing happens when we are free of the obscuring screens of our personal reactions, or our ego investment in an outcome. This enlightened seeing is appreciating reality with mindfulness, that is, without the agendas of or instructions from the conditioned mind or from an ego governed by fear or desire. It is a clean contact with reality, an ineradicable aptitude inherent in every human psyche.

We hear from four teachers who recognized this enlightening fact:

The Spanish mystic Saint John of the Cross says, "Swiftly, with nothing spared, I [ego] am being completely dismantled."

The mystic poet William Blake writes that he must let go of everything "lest the judgment come and find me unannihilate and I be delivered into the hands of my own selfhood."

The bodhisattva says, "I vow to free those who are afraid of the external phenomena that are their own projections."

The Jewish philosopher Martin Buber wrote that God asks Adam, "Where art thou?" not because God does not know, but to help Adam notice his own whereabouts: "Adam hides himself to avoid rendering accounts, to escape responsibility for his way of living. Every person hides for this purpose, for everyone is Adam and finds himself in Adam's situation."

As we do the work of growing in consciousness of our motives and reactions, we discover the many hideouts that keep us from knowing our own whereabouts. Our practice of bringing mindful consciousness to what has been hidden is an alternative to our habit of avoiding, forgetting, or erasing the past through transference of it onto the present. Instead, we can build from it. A hurdle becomes a bridge. A hole becomes an opening. John Donne writes in his poem "The Good Morrow" of how a nowhere becomes a here: "love . . . makes one little room an everywhere."

In a "deficit" model, we see ourselves as needing improvement. This makes sense when it refers to our work on our egos. The fact that perfection is not possible is the psyche's way of protecting us from hubris and inflation. At the same time, we can acknowledge that, from the perspective of our core Self, the repository of archetypal wholeness, we are indeed perfect always and already. John Donne points to this good news in his mystical sonnet on the Annunciation: "That all which always is all everywhere . . . ."

Under the fears and self-recriminations in our ego-minds were and always are pure bliss, pure consciousness, and pure love. The spiritual challenge is not to improve but to allow ourselves to open to what is within and around us. Openness is loving what comes our way as our way. Openness is saying yes to who we are as our path. The eighteenth-century Japanese Zen poet Hakuin, says it this way: "Pointing directly at my human heart, I see my own enlightened nature."

Hidden Help

An unconscious relationship is more powerful
than a conscious one.
—Søren Kierkegaard

Are the tools for working through our transferences only conscious? Can our unconscious also be of help to us on the path to transformation? Psychological work is about making the ego healthy. This means being free enough of fear and confusion that we can achieve our personal goals, live with equanimity in the face of stress, be free of compulsions, and love effectively. Spiritual practice concentrates on letting go of self-centeredness in favor of universal compassion. But ego-dismantling can certainly happen unconsciously too, as in out-of-body moments, near-death experiences, or in other mystical states. This is where deep healing can happen much more powerfully than in talk therapy. We can be open to what may arise in our intuitions, visions, and dreams; paying attention to meaningful coincidences (synchronicity); reading poetry; exploring astrology, *I Ching,* or tarot. We can honor these as ancient archetypal pathways, not simply as forms of divination to satisfy our ego concerns.

We can also make use of body-based therapies that grant us greater contact with our repressed or submerged feelings, sometimes by producing altered states of consciousness. Examples include somatic therapy, intuitive massage, Holotropic Breathwork (developed by the psychiatrist Stanislav Grof), or the process of rebirthing, which can be helpful in reaching the profound unexpressed emotions locked in our subconscious (the unacknowledged emotions that get acted out in our transferences). When our emotions erupt in highly charged ways, they release themselves from their imprisonment in our bodies and move out into the atmosphere, where they dissolve. This is because the full release of an emotion leads to its evaporation. What was held in a constricted space—repressed in our bodies—now opens up through our bodies. We open in order to release. The result of opening is always a letting go.

Thus, we find an answer to our question about how our unconscious can help transform transference. The interior journey toward freedom from transferences is composed of three phases: We move *from* ego *through* the unconscious *to* fuller consciousness.

It is a truly heroic journey, because we take leave of our encapsulation in ego, pass through conscious awareness, and then come back to where we began, but in a more awakened, enlivened state. A heroine brings the light she has found to others. The light is the light of consciousness. We do this also because when we are free of domination by our transferences, we relate more clearly to others, so they share in our release from defense and illusion. Then the heroic cycle from past to present is complete.

To work on all this requires effort and initiative. But we can also respect the "open and flow" potential in us, what Taoists call *wu wei*, the energy of allowing, letting things happen, nondoing, noninterfering, a receptiveness to what may occur. This is a letting in of the unexpected as a guest of grace rather than fearing it as an intruder. We also pay attention to dreams in which family figures or childhood memories morph into the shape of life today. In dreams the unconscious joins us in evoking the raw materials of transference. In this way, our unconscious can assist us, not just cause trouble for us by transferring old feelings onto new people. It is a style that takes the courage of risking openness to forces beyond our control. Then transference opens like a long-shut window, and we finally look through the daylight reality of who we are and who others are too. The good news is that what we see is never so bad as what we thought.

How It All Comes Together

When the pain of continuing our old patterns is greater than the pain of stepping out of them, we are ready for the liberation of ego and the enlightenment of mind. Anais Nin says it this way in her *Diary:* "There came a time when staying tight within the bud became more painful than the risk it took to bloom."

We see that remaining stuck in unconscious motivation and projection is itself a form of pain. That pain is sharper than the pain of letting ourselves become conscious of our real story and how we can move past it. Physical pain is best attended to early on, before it affects our neural pathways and becomes chronic. This is why unconscious transference has a strike against it: we usually allow it to go on for so long that it becomes chronic.

How does psychological work on transference become integrated into our spiritual practices? We remind ourselves that to handle something with psychological tools is to address, process, resolve, and integrate what has happened to us. For instance, if a partner leaves us for someone else, we admit that we are hurt, see our part in it, go through our feelings of grief (sadness, anger, fear), notice how what has just happened is picking up extra weight because it is repeating the felt sense of abandonment from our childhood, resolve to get on with life without blaming our partner, and finally choose to form healthy relationships in the future.

Healing, in medical terms, is simply a return to normal functioning, or freedom from symptoms. We can see psychological healing in a deeper way: healing as the recovery of wholeness, whether or not symptoms persist. Healing in this context is restoration of balance. We do not find this healing by willpower or by clearing everything up neatly. We find it by opening—the etiquette for spiritual experiences. Healing seems to happen best when we open to our own psychospiritual reality, the reality of ourselves in balance.

Here is an example of a spiritually conscious response within a relationship: A partner says or does something to us that is mean and hurtful. In loving-kindness, we feel sadness for him and then say with sincere compassion, either directly or internally, "Oh, what terrible things must have happened to you in your past that would make you say/do something this mean." When we respond this way, we show that protecting our own ego is no longer our main concern in our relationship; loving-kindness is. At the same time, if words become abusive, we can stand up for ourselves in a nonaggressive way. If dialogue is impossible, we run for shelter while feeling compassion in our hearts.

Practice
Opening to Spiritual Shifts

Loving-kindness happens best as we deconstruct our neurotic ego, which is ruled by what in Buddhism are called the three poisons: greed, hate, and delusion. They are resistances to what is, obstacles to enlightenment. In greed, we possess and cling to what we want; in hate, we destroy or avoid what we don't want; in delusion, we believe that to have what we want will give us lasting happiness and to avoid what we don't want will give us lasting security.

We can transform these errant but natural inclinations into skillful means toward growth: Greed becomes reaching out to grasp, but only that which is good for us. Hate becomes taking a stand against injustice, but only in nonviolent ways. Delusion becomes the healthy imagination that allows us to believe in a world beyond our story. This is how we might hit upon a spiritual exit from the toils of any ego snare.

Here are some practices that can help us to integrate our psychological and spiritual work:

1. Instead of simply relying on self-improvement techniques or on our skills in implementing them, we ask for help from saints and bodhisattva guides. This acknowledges the limitations of ego efforts and psychological answers and opens us to the constant availability of grace, the archetype of the assisting force within and around us all. This is the power that makes us stretch beyond our ego's limited efforts and knowledge to the far reaches of effectiveness and wisdom.

2. We sit mindfully with what happens in our relationships, that is, in the pure experience of the here and now, without intrusion by the mind-sets of ego. This is a way of opening to reality and making space for it without being inhibited by our fears of what we might not be able to handle and our fixations on what we feel compelled to possess.

3. We say yes unconditionally to this reality just as it is and to the people around us just as they are. We affirm and accept the truth of impermanence, the danger of attachment, and the importance of making a deeper commitment to the conscientious path, the path with heart.

4. We act with loving-kindness and forgo retaliation of any kind, especially toward those who instigated our transferences. We beam loving-kindness not only to those now in our life story but

to any people anywhere who are now facing the same issues we are. This establishes a conscious connection with all humanity, the very thing we always wanted and without which there is no safety in the world, as history keeps showing us so ruthlessly and ineluctably. The barriers we usually place between those we love and those we dislike disappear in loving-kindness, since we wish them all equal happiness. In this sense, loving-kindness is immeasurable.

5. We say and show thanks for the graces that helped us to sit mindfully in our pain, handle it effectively, and find an opening through it.

6. Ongoing commitment to meditation rounds out our spiritual practices. In mindfulness meditation we struggle and surrender. We put energy into sitting in a way that creates the best context for success in meditating and we surrender to the fact of our constant distractions. Our success is in the continual starting over. This a metaphor for doing the work, both psychologically and spiritually. We perform our practices and we accept the fact of our embarrassing failures. All that matters is that we pick ourselves up one more time than we fall down, try one more time than we fail, go on one more time than we back away.

These six spiritual practices put the finishing touches on what psychological work can only inaugurate. On the other hand, without doing the psychological work, these practices may fail to take lasting hold or to help us know ourselves and to learn from what happens to us. The psychological work is not enough; the spiritual practices are not enough. To be fully human is to cultivate not only psychological health but our spiritual potentials too.

The path to no-self—a sense of ourselves as connected and contingent rather than separate and ruggedly independent—passes through the sane ego. Instead of self or no-self as a distinction, we may want to look at how we have become attached versus how we can let go. Then we see that the path to the no-self of freedom from attachment passes through the sane ego. It became sane by letting go of its fears and cravings. The path to a stable sense of ourselves results in liberation from being caught in ego. This is why healing happens so well when we are faithful both to our psychological work and to our spiritual practice as we attempt to finalize an experience.

The results of practice are themselves spiritual commitments:

- I become an observer of others, while yet being curious and caring.
- I take what happens or what is said as information rather than egoically/personally as I have in the past.
- I continue to be affected by others' behavior while at the same time my serenity remains intact.
- I am no longer provoked and devastated by others, only touched and excited.
- I align myself to what happens rather than attempting to twist it into what gratifies or consoles me.
- I act lovingly no matter how I am treated, and, at the same time, I do not tolerate abuse of any kind.
- I am thankful for how my practice and my guides have come through for me.

Grace certainly shows us that we do not have to rely only on people for need-fulfillment.

When love is my only defense, I am invincible.
　　　　　　　　　—Tao Te Ching

14

Transferring beyond the Personal

The journey with father and mother up and down many ladders represents the making conscious of infantile contents that have not yet been integrated . . . . This personal unconscious must always be dealt with first . . . . otherwise the gateway to the cosmic unconscious cannot be opened.

—Carl Jung

For Freud the unconscious is personal, the result of the repression of memories. Jung proposes, in addition, an inborn collective unconscious shared by all humans, hence transpersonal. Personal and transpersonal are not two realms. Our personal life experience is simply where the transpersonal dimension of our psyche manifests.

Personal transference finds its sources in the figures of our personal life, for example, our own mother and father. Some of our memories/expectations of them reside in our personal unconscious, and this leads to transference in later life.

Each of us is a unique articulation of a vast archetypal world, so we sometimes experience feelings that do not arise from our own biography but from that of the human family. In our collective unconscious we carry symbols and characters shared by all human societies. They include, for instance, an earth mother and a sky father. These collective archetypes/prototypes may also become sources of transference by us onto others or by others onto us. We may unconsciously see our spouse as an earth mother who will nurture and protect us. A group may see the face of a hero in its leader with the hope that he will be a reliable protector. As a nation, we might see the villainous or demonic shadow in those we fear or hate, a dangerous game that can justify our resorting to violence or war.

We might notice that our sense of being under threat by our manager at work resembles the feeling we had toward our own father. In that case we are picking up on a personal transference. Sometimes, the feeling upgrades in us so that fear of being fired becomes a terror of impending doom. When that happens, we may be experiencing an archetypal transference, one that comes from our inherited dread of death, judgment, and Armageddon.

In positive transference, these same concepts apply. Our admiration or reverence for someone may be based on how she resembles the aunt who raised us. Or she may assume superhuman qualities, evoking a collective transference based on the earth-mother archetype. In such an instance, we have invested someone with goddess energy and are overlooking the fact that she may make the same mistakes anyone would or disappoint us as anyone can. The more we transfer or project, the more do we ignore the given of universal inadequacy. Our paradoxical condition can become a spiritual aspiration: "May I widen my circle of compassion, let go of expectations, and accept others in all their wonderfully rich humanity."

The Archetypes We Live With

Just as all our human bodies have a similar physical anatomy, so does our psyche. It contains universal and perennial motifs. These are the archetypes, the innate energies in the collective psyche. They are depicted in imagination, stories, myths, and dreams. They are recognizable and meaningful to all of us. For example, the cast of characters in stories are archetypes recognizable the world over: hero, villain, mother, father, king, queen, helping and hurting forces, wise guides, tricksters, wounded healers, and so on. Many of the common themes of stories, especially religious stories, are also archetypes, such as resurrection, ascension, reincarnation, revelation, judgment, initiation, afterlife, karma, salvation.

The scriptures of all religions are likewise powerful, because they echo our collective primal fears and desires. They threaten punishment for our sins and promise us rewards in heaven. We may notice that the archetypal level appeals to the primitive side of humanity as well as to the evolving side. No matter how sophisticated we have become, we still carry the ancient superstitions and terrors of our ancestors and we project them onto likely candidates, especially those with authority.

The objects of our archetypal fascination, especially in religious devotion, can evoke an archetypal transference. We can find the mother who unconditionally loves us in the Virgin Mary or Kuan Yin (goddess of compassion); we can fear the enemy/abuser in the form of Satan or the demon Mara of Buddhist lore. The archetype of the wise guide can show itself to us as a bodhisattva, guardian angel, or Holy Spirit.

Films and stories, both mythic and religious, have impact and meaning in direct proportion to how strongly they present us with archetypal characters and themes. *The Wizard of Oz, Star Wars, The Matrix,* and *Harry Potter* stand out in our imaginations precisely because of their success at blending archetypal story, characters, and subject. This is appealing to us since, while watching these films, we are actually looking into our own inner world with all its potentials. As a group, the archetypes reflect the soul's innate and full capacities.

A downside in archetypal transference is that we might thereby deny the potential of a hero, or any archetype, in ourselves. We fail to see the light or the shadow in ourselves when we adore or deplore those of others. A client may look up to her therapist as the source of wisdom and overlook her own powers of discernment. A spouse may dislike or feel threatened by his unfaithful partner for manifesting the archetype of the trickster, one that is actually present but hidden in himself.

In personal transference there is something incomplete that requires attention. In collective transference the same thing happens. The collective unconscious is wholeness, that is, containing all the archetypal energies of all humanity and a perfect combination of all apparent opposites. In a life ruled by the competing fears and desires of ego, we fail to enter the wholeness of these powers. This is registered in the psyche as incompleteness, a failure to measure up to the larger life beyond ego that wants to burst out in us always and everywhere.

We can tell when a personal transference has become archetypal because it seems bigger than fits the situation or greater than fits ordinary human traits, good or bad. For example, an authority figure upon whom we have unconsciously projected the archetype of the divine judge calls us on our misdeeds or on our selfishness toward him. We cannot seem to make enough amends. We feel our remorse with a sense that we will be punished in some harsh way, even though he is not threatening that. We are at the mercy of an archetype that is as vast as that of the Last Judgment that plagued the medieval imagination.

Here is another example of archetypes at work in transference: A child may not have been nurtured by her parents because they were absent emotionally, especially because of alcoholism or mental illness. As a result, she found herself needed in the family as a parental substitute, caretaking her younger siblings, or even her parents at times. She herself then becomes the parent while being also parentless, an orphan. The common and dangerous triangle of the three archetypes—child, mother, and orphan—can lead to confusion in adult life about one's role in a marriage. Am I the parent here? Have I despaired of getting my child-needs met? Am I trying too hard to get them met by my partner? When do I get my turn to have a childhood, or am I wrong to expect one? The confusion of personal and archetypal may account for many conflicts in relationships.

Archetypal themes are predispositions that make us value or be drawn to some things more than to others. We may then design our life accordingly. For instance, one person may value books if her natural disposition is toward the scholar or wisdom archetype. One person is endowed from birth with a natural talent for art and another with a fascination for and knowledge of herbal healing. The person with a talent for sports or mechanics feels almost compelled to practice his hand at them. We all contain all the archetypes. Yet, since specific ones are central in each of us, archetypes can point us to our calling. Indeed, our deepest needs, values, and wishes reflect which particular archetypes are strongest in us. Our life purpose works out for the best when we live out the energies of the unique archetypes we were born to articulate. This connection between our passion and our purpose is called the fulfillment of destiny.

Our life has come to us across the generations and on its way it gathered beliefs, myths, and fears that have enduring and imposing dimensions. We never grow out of our past, not personally, not collectively. That does not have to frighten or depress us. We can notice it and work with it. Just having this information about ourselves helps us identify our vulnerability to archetypal transferences, and that is the step of addressing that initiates the work.

Acknowledge or Disavow Our Wholeness?

The basis of human hope lies in the fact that the psyche never gives up on us. Something in us wants us to restore ourselves to wholeness, so we are endowed with an urge for it. Deep in our collective unconscious is an organismic integrity that the object relations theorist Margaret Mahler calls "an innate given, a thrust toward individuation which seems to continue during the entire life cycle." In other words, we are geared to articulate in our lifetime more and more of our wholeness. Our part of the task is our work. The result Jung called individuation: "becoming the self you were intended to be."

Emma Jung, the wife of Carl Jung, described its urgency: "An inner wholeness presses its still unfulfilled claims upon us." The Dalai Lama expresses this same idea: "The capacity for positive transformation lies naturally within the constitution of the mind itself." Phrases like "we are geared," "intended to be," "inner wholeness," "naturally within" show that something about us is a gift. All we have to do is open it. Grace is at work in us on our path to individuation. This is why we never give up on ourselves, or on others either. Our work is not striving for change as much as aligning ourselves to its unfolding. We can trust that wholeness wants to happen. All through life it will not let up or give up on us. Wholeness is like an unconditional love.

An enlightened voice within us clamors for transcendence of ego, for spiritual wholeness. When we transfer or project archetypal powers onto others, we are acknowledging that inner voice, but we are stopping at its personifications as represented by others rather than opening it in ourselves. This is how the archetype of wholeness—a combination of both our light and our dark side—remains unacknowledged in us. We recall John Keats's "Ode to Melancholy":

Aye, in the very temple of Delight
Veiled melancholy has her sovereign shrine.

If, instead of projecting wholeness and virtue onto others, we project meanness and evil, thereby denying our own positive potentials as well, it is much more dangerous to the world than any individual destructive actions we might take. It is useful to bear in mind that all those who have done evil or have shown goodness began with the same potential for them as we have now.

Once greatness is understood as existing outside ourselves, up there on the throne, we diminish our trust in our own inner wisdom and hand our minds over to those who may misuse them. Once evil is only outside us, war, genocide, retaliation, torture, hate crimes, and mass destruction are justified. As we withdraw our projections and acknowledge our transferences, we take steps toward retrieving our own wholeness.

In a positive archetypal transference by others onto us, we are seen as godlike or as the all-knowing guru. The challenge is to forgo taking these kudos personally and thereby feeling an inflated sense of our own power. Instead, we encourage the other to give his praise to the Buddha or Christ or to the divine nature within us all, our spiritual identity beyond ego: "What you admire in me is in you too." We have all seen the pope, definitely a source of collective transference, on the balcony at Saint Peter's. As the people cheer him, he raises both arms and continually lifts his hands toward the sky. This is his way of saying, "Do not cheer and praise me as a person but lift all that praise to God in heaven." This is the pope's recommendation to the crowd to put an end to the transference onto him and reroute it in its proper direction.

People may transfer the collective negative archetypal powers of the villain/shadow onto us. They may see us as miscreants to be punished, orphans to be abandoned, heretics to be excluded, ogres to be annihilated. As members of the human collective, we will automatically feel terror at any judgment of us that has such archetypal dimensions. That terror is a signal to be cautious and not foolhardy. Some cunning people deliberately foster that reaction. They seem more authoritative in their demagoguery than they really are. Our work is to notice this posturing and not be caught in its manipulations.

We can, in those moments, also call upon the archetypal primal powers available to us in bodhisattvas and saints. As Jung says, "Whoever speaks in primordial images evokes the beneficent forces that ever and anon have enabled humanity to find a refuge from every peril and to outlive its longest night." This is again the archetype of spiritual support called grace, free assistance beyond what effort can engineer.

In summary, we now see how the wholeness of the psyche works by combining two directions:

The personal unconscious is:	*The collective unconscious is:*
Blank pages that soon become a family album	An innate and ageless world library of art and wisdom
Built on experiences with family members	A container of archetypes that are universal across human cultures
Revealed in personally`oriented dreams and in personal transferences	Revealed in collectively oriented dreams and archetypal transferences
Moved by desire for relationship with special persons	Moved by a spiritual longing for connectedness with all that is
Holding an inner child that is unique in each of us	Contained in a Divine Child, an archetype identical in all of us
A narrative and cellular memory that remains in us and is triggered by what happens in relationships so that transferences result	An instinctive memory that endures within the human collective and appears to us at special times so that revelations can happen

The Example of Patriotism

Patriotism comes from the same Latin word as *father*. Blind patriotism is collective transference. In it the state becomes a parent and we citizens submit our loyalty to ensure its protection. We may have been encouraged to make that bargain from our public school education, our family home, religion, or culture in general. We associate safety with obedience to authority, for example, going along with government policies. We then make duty, as it is defined by the nation, our unquestioned course. Our motivation is usually not love of country but fear of being without a country that will defend us and our property. Connection is all-important to us; excommunication is the equivalent of death, the finality we can't dispute. Healthy adult loyalty is a virtue that does not become blind obedience for fear of losing connection, nor total devotion so that we lose our boundaries.

Our civil obedience can be so firm that it may take precedence over our concern for those we love, even our children. Here is an example: A young mother is told by the doctor that her toddler is allergic to peanuts and peanut oil. She lets the school know of her son's allergy when he goes to kindergarten. Throughout his childhood, she is vigilant and makes sure he is safe from peanuts in any form. Eighteen years later, there is a war and he is drafted. The same mother, who was so scrupulously careful about her child's safety, now waves goodbye to him with a tear *but without protest.* Mother's own training in public school and throughout her life has made her believe that her son's life is expendable whether or not the war in question is just. "Patriotism" is so deeply ingrained in her that she does not even imagine an alternative, even when her son's life is at stake.

It is of course also true that, biologically, parents are ready to let children go just as the state is ready to draft them. What a cunning synchronicity. In addition, old men who decide on war take advantage of the timing too. The warrior archetype is lively in eighteen-year-olds, who are willing to fight. Those in their mid-thirties, whose archetype is being a householder and making a mark in their chosen field, will not show an interest in battlefields of blood. The chiefs count on the fact that young braves will take the warrior myth literally rather than as a metaphor for interior battles. They will be willing to put their lives on the line to live out the collective myth of societies that have not found the path of nonviolence. Our collective nature thus seems geared to making war a workable enterprise. In some people, peacemaking is the archetype most in evidence. Nature seems to have made that population smaller, unfortunately.

Our culture has trained us to endure and tolerate, not to protest and rebel. Every cell of our bodies learned that lesson. It may not be virtue; it may be fear. We may believe that showing anger is dangerous, because it opposes the authority we are obliged to appease and placate if we are to survive. This explains why we so admire someone who dares to say no and to stand up or even to die for what he believes. That person did not fall prey to the collective seduction.

Watching *Jeopardy* on television, I notice that the audience applauds with special force when a contestant risks everything on a double-jeopardy question. The healthy part of us ardently admires daring. In our positive shadow, our admiration reflects our own disavowed or hidden potential. We, too, have it in us to dare. We can stand up for our truth, putting every comfort on the line, if only we can calm our long-scared ego and open to the part of us that wants to live free. Joseph Campbell says encouragingly, "The part of us that wants to become is fearless."

Religion and Transference

Transference is not simply horizontal, from person to person, but vertical from person to a higher power, usually personified as God. When God is "Our Father," we are likely to transfer onto our image of him the traits of our own father or of the father we wish we had had. When powerful father figures come along, we might see their hand as a divine hand, and do obeisance accordingly. Certainly the Divine Mother can be the mother we missed out on. We might also treat a woman we admire as a Madonna.

Western religion presents the divine in ways that are closely connected to childhood beliefs and fears. Images of a God who rewards us for being good and punishes us for disobedience find a firm footing in the psyche because they are familiar, that is, like family. These themes influence how we relate to our almighty parents and later to partners or authority figures who may awe or intimidate us. Transference comes into play when our relationship to archetypal forces applies to individuals.

It also works in reverse. We see our own parental imagoes in divine images. This is because the divine father and mother are archetypes that reside in the collective human psyche. They can be as real to our psyche as our own parents are. As we saw above, our life is conditioned not only by our own families but by our innate inheritance from the human family.

The danger lies in superstition: irrational beliefs that grow into fear, self-negation, or the justification of aggression. Healthy adult faith is not grounded in such magical thinking but in discernment of how religious values can enrich our lives and our relationship to society. This will include a divesting of our parents' image from God and our God image from our parents. Then a personal relationship to God can emerge, a devotion free of transference.

When our image of God resembles that of our own father, it becomes possible to believe that God is love and yet punitive too. That contradiction was visible in our own father, so it comes as no surprise in God. Indeed, for some of us, the crucifix made this transaction seem legitimate: the Father has a right to hurt his son, since he loves him.

Our image of God reflects parenting patterns. As parents become more kindly, God becomes less frightening. "Come, let us reason together" (Isa. 1:18) then supersedes "A fire is kindled by my anger" (Deut. 32:22). The image of a father today is more kindly than in past generations, but our own inner image of God as father may not yet reflect this update in gentleness. Our sense of God may come from the archetype of the severe, unbending taskmaster, reflecting the father of past generations. His love is conditional. His rules have to be followed, because father knows best. These rules are absolute and not necessarily tailored to our own personal qualities, needs, and predicaments. In fact, in the patriarchal view, relativism is immoral and dangerous. The accent is on the "either... or," "good or bad." The attitude of the strict father or leader is "You are either with me or against me." There is a guaranteed punishment if his rules are not obeyed.

Religion may proclaim that the rules of a judging/punishing God are divinely revealed and indisputable. Our faith tasks are only to know them and to obey them. To oversee this, there is an established patriarchal authority: *men* deputized to teach and supervise us. They might declare that uniformity is necessary to preserve orthodoxy or for us to save our souls, but the goal might actually be to keep us under their control. Transference works against us in this kind of immature religious view: we become vulnerable to fear of challenging an established hierarchy when it resembles our authoritative father.

The negative shadow side of patriarchy is in its exclusivity: there is always someone who is inside and someone who is outside. Membership is crucial to survival, since being in the fold offers the unique and only access to graces and consolations that are so necessary to equip us for the perils of the world. The authority figures who impose their rules upon us under threat of punishment resemble the retaliatory ego more than a God of love, compassion, and generosity.

The threat of being censured for our sins may instill a fear that we will be rejected and shunned by those upon whom we rely for support, including support beyond the grave. A patriarchal structure, for example, an established church, might exploit our primitive fear of breaking the rules. We then feel too afraid to speak up or to question authority because of the threat of penalty, especially that of being on the outside. We fail to trust the Holy Spirit that blows where she will—the same Spirit who is freedom from separateness, who has actually breathed away the fiction of inside versus outside and who has made all of us worthy.

Some religious teachings capitalize on fostering an ongoing sense of sin and unworthiness to keep us in line. They become invitations to transference if they remind us of parents who were overly critical or were punitive toward us for stepping outside the margins, the only space in which unique identity is possible. (There old images fade in the light of what is new.)

Our discussion reminds us of what Carl Jung once asked: "Who is the awe-inspiring guest who knocks at our door so portentously?" The guest who does not arise from our usual storehouse of images knocks with the force of destiny. This guest is not made in the image of our parents. This guest is not a projection of the ego's wish to dominate or punish. This guest is not a transference from or onto any person, place, or thing. Rather, this guest has hailed from the transpersonal world within and around us. This guest is the awe to which we can bow, the knock that we allow ourselves to hear, the door that we finally open into surprising passages and presages.

The higher self is just such a door, as is Buddha mind, Christ consciousness, or any religious path that commits us to follow our bliss and act with love. It is the door that Joseph Campbell says "opens where we thought there was no door." It was only the limited ego, with its characteristic fear and sense of scarcity, that could ever have come up with the concept of "no door." Beyond such a thought and beyond transferences is the door that we really are, the opening into the divine heart of the universe. The philosopher Martin Heidegger tells us our name: "Persons are not things or processes but openings through which the infinite manifests."

Light and Dark

In the Hebrew Bible, the fact that David turns to God for help when he is attacked by other humans (Ps. 22:1 and 38:3) is an acknowledgment that malevolence from others may not be experienced as personal only, but as having transpersonal proportions. In our interactions with others we are sometimes dealing, as the heroes were, with mythic forces of cosmic proportions. Saint Paul seems to be referring to this archetypal shadow when he writes, "Our battle is not with flesh and blood but against powers and principalities, against the world rulers of this present darkness, against spiritual forces . . . ." (Eph. 6:12) The dark side of humanity is often personified as a devil. He is feared as cajoling us into temptation and preparing a place of endless punishment for us in his hell realm. This is a negative collective transference that still seems to capture and fascinate the human imagination.

Collective transference appears positively in religion too. For instance, we may notice the similarity between our own childhood experience and the archetype of the Divine Child, who suffers and is unwelcome but survives nonetheless, thanks to divine aid. In this respect, the theme of the hero as an endangered infant is personified in Jesus, Moses, Dionysus, and Horus, all of whom have a similar story. We, too, are vulnerable in early life and not always safe or welcome. Yet grace came our way in the form of people who loved us in ways that helped us grow to maturity.

When we are fascinated by the myths, are we not transferring our own saga onto the stories of heroes? Are we not recognizing that to do the work it takes to have a healthy adulthood can be the same as the heroic journey of saints and heroes? The divine archetypes can become assisting forces through our positive transferences. Such projections are not simply illusions. They can lead to healthy transferences that grant us contact with the assisting forces of grace in the image of a caring God, a compassionate Buddha, a guardian angel, and so on. The sense of security that results in us leads us to an adult faith in which we parent and guard ourselves *with* a sense of accompaniment too. Then healthy religious transference is a bridge, not a harbor.

With the aid of divine forces, our work is clearly no longer simply psychological but spiritual too. For instance, fear cannot be a secular phenomenon only, because ultimately it ushers us toward powers that seem able and willing to help us with resources of courage beyond our ordinary limitations. This is how the collective transferences are worked through by access to transcendent powers, those beyond ego. We can understand how the belief in a heaven "up there" arose in the human heart, since kindly forces seem so lofty that they must live in a realm above our heads.

Transference in religion thrives on the similarity of function between parent and church. By rituals and sacraments a church shows that it accompanies us throughout life as a guiding and nurturant parent. Rituals are performed at important times in life, such as birth, coming of age, marriage, death—all the times at which our parents and partners are with us too. Transference onto a church and its authority will thus certainly happen in such rituals of welcome, initiation, relationship commitment, and leave-taking. This is because our crucial thresholds are appearing in the context of a holding community and in the arms of an archetypal mother church. The comfort and loyalty of a religion also reminds us of the similar virtues we found in our own kindly parents or partners.

Finally, we might turn to a familiar example from childhood to see how a common transference of childhood can develop into spiritual insight. Santa Claus is a fantasy character (though his image is based on an actual person, Saint Nicholas, a Turkish bishop). Santa Claus does two things: he gives us gifts and he arrives at our home in some mysterious way. In these ways, he is a transference figure both personally and collectively. He represents our own parents and our trust in a supernatural Parent, both of whom, we believe, see to it that we are provided for.

At first, in early childhood, we believe in Santa Claus literally. Then, as we grow up, we understand that our parents give us our holiday gifts and there is no magic involved in that. However, at another level we appreciate that gifts are an expression of generosity and are not an obligation. As we grow in spiritual maturity, we discover that this is a metaphor for the religious notion of grace: a gift that comes to us from beyond human making but, fortunately for us, is not based on whether or not we are deserving. We then see that gifts, especially those at Christmas or on birthdays, are concrete articulations of the archetype of the gift dimension of life. We also see that the archetype of grace, like Santa, indeed arrives at our home—or into ourselves—in mysterious ways. Thus we come full circle to the deeper meaning of the archetype of Santa Claus, who is essentially a personification of exactly that reality. So we were not that far off to begin with!

Santa Claus, when taken literally, is a fantasy character with a historical origin. Santa Claus as a metaphor is an archetypal reality whose historical origin does not matter, because its power is in the truth and mystery of grace that comes to us daily. Santa Claus personifies an important spiritual teaching: neither death nor life, nor principalities, nor powers can keep us from a love that comes to us from a friendly universe.

> *The world of mountains and rivers, of bread and wine, of friends and enemies, is all held and displayed in the universal monstrance, the Showing, the phenomenalization of the Absolute. This is, as far as I can see, what the Mysteries, in their various mythic forms and traditions, are trying to tell us.*
> —Beatrice Bruteau

EPILOGUE

A Jungian View of
Our Larger Life

In *The Psychology of the Transference,* Carl Jung shows that the characteristics of the transference/countertransference dynamic seem to represent an alchemical conjunction of apparent opposites: ego and Self, ourselves and others, life and death, love and aggression. *Alchemical* refers to the transformation of ordinary elements into spiritual realities, or of an ego into the higher self. Transference and countertransference may be our attempts to do this alchemical work, since within a dyad of transference people experience opposites in one another as similarities. Indeed, polarities *attract* their opposite.

A successful relationship is one in which each partner learns to deal with the tension of opposites by staying with it and bringing it into awareness so that a common bond can be formed or strengthened. The tension of opposites is where our lively energy resides. We engage with contradictions to find the path into soulful intimacy, both within ourselves and in relationship. At the alchemical/spiritual level, we may be in conflict *in order to* coalesce. This can be a painful process, but it results in growth and ever-increasing clarity about one another. It is ironic in this regard that the word *compatible* comes from a Latin word meaning "to suffer together." As we endure our mutual transferences, compatibility begins to happen in every sense of the word.

Transference also sets up a *temenos*, a transformational field, a sacred space in which we find ourselves out and evolve from deep inside. The room we are in with our friend or partner or workmate is like a ritual enclosure, a temple of contemplation. Larger-than-life images and realities come into play as we interact, seemingly only as individuals. In reality, archetypal forces are peering at us through the faces of ordinary folk. To work through transference is to deconstruct the mighty archetypal powers behind appearances. Almost everyone who has become significant to us has somehow come to represent archetypal themes. As we deconstruct those meanings, the people reduce to life-size, rather than inflate to god-size, and we can be together with more ease.

Thus, the ultimate working through of our collective transference is to recover divinity from the gods, to see the Buddha as personifying our own enlightenment, to see every grand personage as a mirror of ourselves, both for light and for dark. Then we have returned to that sense of connection we have been longing for since our first parents became exiles from the paradise of uncomplicated love.

Our sense of fulfillment is no longer tied to narrow ego-satisfactions but to our soul's ever-expanding yearning to beam the light we are. Then we walk into our lives and relationships with a contented smile and gift-bestowing hands.

> *You are a child of the universe no less than the trees and the stars; you have a right to be here. Whether or not it is clear to you, no doubt the universe is unfolding as it should . . . . With all its sham, drudgery, and broken dreams, it is still a beautiful world.*
> —Max Ehrmann